A. ROSS
& T. ROSS

WORTH MORE THAN A THOUSAND WORDS

People fear the monster on the street,
not the one in the house

Acknowledgments

"God is great, God is good…"

I grew up hearing those words daily while sitting with my family at the dinner table.

On Sundays with extended family, we would sing old hymns like, "Praise to the Lord, The Almighty the King of Creation, O My soul Praise Him for He is Thy Health and Salvation…"

I thank my Almighty God for overcoming the evil in this world. Jesus came to conquer that evil with His unconditional love. Jesus was the smartest, kindest, most unselfish being that ever walked this earth and ever will walk this earth. Thank you, Jesus, for being our example of how we should love others. Thank you for giving me the gift of eternity with You, a mansion in heaven where happiness, joy, and peace are forever in the company of everyone that God is willing to save that wants to be saved from eternal punishment.

Regarding this true story, I thank The Happy Guy Writers Team for help with forming chapter after chapter. They helped form the backbone of the book. I had to get the meat and fat on those bones with informational details. I appreciate your patience and encouragement along the way.

Thank you to Exodus Christian Design for numerous, careful hours creating the book cover design, editing, and beautiful interior book formatting.

Thank you, "quietSundays" on Fiverr, for your beta reading services and for coming up with a catchy subtitle for this book.

Thank you, my eldest daughter, for freely sharing your part of the story. May almighty God bless you with friends and financial support because of this book.

To my dear daughters and grandson: I pray that you will feel how very much God loves and cares for you! May God's Spirit of Love, Joy, Peace, Patience, Kindness, Goodness, Faithfulness, Gentleness, and Self-Control be with you forever and forever! Thank you to my late parents and grandparents for molding me into who I am today. Thank you, Mom, and Sister, for being a listening ear on the phone while my little family was in chaos. You helped me by being there!

Thank you to my dear extended family and old friends for your friendship and great memories.

Thank you, dear readers, for your interest in this story. May you learn things you never knew before. We all can be better problem solvers with intellectual ammunition. God bless you all and keep you forever in His eternal care!

Table of Contents

Introduction

As parents, we are supposed to make sure our children get a better life than we have, right?

I wanted to share our dysfunctional family's story to educate others interested in knowing and hopefully solving the age-old problem of incest. At first, I intended each of us to tell our part of the story. With no hesitation at all, Tia volunteered to tell her story. My Ana refused. "Mom, it's such a sad story!" she exclaimed. Much more of my ex-husband's side of the story would have been interesting. He made absolutely no comment whatsoever about my idea. I recently learned that it was too depressing for him to talk about his time in prison.

If you compare how I grew up to how my daughters grew up, you can understand why I would feel guilty about how great most of my childhood was! Sure, I was bothered by my indifferent, silent, stern father, and my daughters' childhoods would have been quite pleasant if their father had been appropriately physically distant like my father.

I had many happy memories. Misery was a constant companion for my daughters, and I learned this after their father went to prison.

Years later, I realized how blessed I was with my upbringing! I certainly wanted my children to have a better life than mine!

I saw Tia's cute stick man drawing every time I walked up and down the stairwell. She had erased a very intimate detail on the stick man. If only I would have asked her lots of questions about it! She told me surprising information over 20 years after drawing that cute little fat stick man. She explained that it was her father. She had erased his private part.

I want to caution sensitive readers and forewarn them that there are disturbing graphic details in some of these accounts. I recommend this writing only for mature readers.

How can an individual make use of a horrible chain of events? Tell the story, educate others, and make friends. Start a club. A terrible event can help those who want to learn about tragedy. It is like turning scraps of cloth into a beautiful quilt. Broken glass can turn into pretty ceramics. Lovely! Clams make an irritating rock into stunning pearls. Pretty! We can make delicious, sweet lemonade out of sour lemons. Yummy! Moose manure makes exciting artwork. For real! Cow, Horse, or Rabbit manure can help plants grow big. True! Artists make jewelry from bird droppings! A crappy story can teach others what abuse is! (Some names have been changed in this story.)

CHAPTER 1
Farm Raised

I was born by cesarean section to a mother with type-one diabetes at age four. Doctors said she probably would not live past 12, but they were wrong. After my birth, the family doctor strongly urged Mom not to have more children. But she was determined that I would not be a spoiled, only child. She had a miscarriage before my sister came along.

Early Years

I developed an interest in exploring the boundaries of my existence and trying new things. I grew up on a small-scale Holstein dairy and grain farm in southwest Minnesota, and my dad's parents lived next door. I felt blessed even before I knew the meaning of the word! During my toddler years, the most stable part of my life was when I had all four grandparents living nearby.

When I was a toddler, my St. Bernard, Snowby, and I took a long walk to the gravel pit on the south edge of the farm, which was soon out of sight. Fortunately, a neighbor threshing out in the field saw us, picked me up, and brought Snowby and me back home on the tractor, safe and sound. Oh, how I enjoyed the adventure of exploration and discovery!

Snowby and I went for our usual leisurely walk around the barnyard in another incident. Near one of the outlying barns, we came across what I thought was "Peter Rabbit," a skunk that Snowby and I met only one time on our daily explorations. Snowby ran to dunk her head in her water pail by the farmyard hydrant. The skunk sprayed on us and ran away! Mom had a problem getting the skunk smell out of my clothes.

My parents put up a strong metal chain-link fence to keep Snowby and me from wandering away so we could be safe.

I developed into a verbal child early in my toddler years. My silent, angry father (later diagnosed with PTSD from the Korean Conflict) snapped at me often when I spoke, effectively silencing me. I learned to keep a low, passive profile. I avoided expressing heartfelt emotions or strong beliefs. To this day, hauntingly quiet people scare me!

A popular song called "The Elephant Walk" would play on KWOA. Mom continually played the radio from dawn until dusk. At dusk, we would hear the instrumental melody of the hymn, "Now the Day is over, night is drawing nigh…" Then they would go off the air.

In the dining room, a tiny yellowish ceramic wall hanging was above the stereo and the old 1950s radio with a Bible verse that read, "Be still and know that I am God." Grandpa H. and his brothers built our house in the 1920s. Solid oak was all over the interior. There was an elegant buffet on the west side of the dining room with a big mirror that I used to stare at when I sat at the dining table. Above the mirror was a two feet high by six feet wide window with wood lattices. We could see the tall apple trees on that side. Above the fireplace in the living room, we would stand and admire the solid oak wood carving that Grandma H. made during her engagement to Grandpa. It said,

"East, West, Hames Best." I often wondered about the "a" in Hames, and I was sure it was a misspelled word or a particularly fancy "o." On the north side wall, we had a carved Bible verse that Grandma H. made that said, "I can do all things through Christ who strengthens me." Each of her five children got a different Bible verse carved for them.

Every Sunday, we would go to the Presbyterian Church. In 1918 the beautiful old church was built. It had colorful stain-glassed windows and solid polished wood rafters. Beautiful, waxed wood covered the floors, and the double doors into the sanctuary were ornamentally carved wood. We sang those beautiful old hymns and spent worship time with extended family. Sometimes after church, there would be many potluck dishes and several varieties to choose from. We children happily ran outside and around the church. Then into the church and back out again. Our families gave us adorations of love. I was a Golden Platinum Blonde fairy child with a mischievous grin and behavior to match. My mom nicknamed me "Suzie Q," and my little sister was "Toady."

An intelligent, fun-loving man, my maternal Grandpa O. loved to tease my grandmother by saying to me in front of her, "You love me more than Grandma, don't you?!" She would scold him in a fun way. I absorbed all the love and nurturing that my grandparents gave me. At age 55, grandpa started a plumbing and heating business. He was quick with math problems. Grandpa had been a land surveyor earlier in his career. He was always carrying around his toolbox. I called it his toy box. I loved how he engaged me in conversations. He would sometimes put mashed potatoes on his ice cream cone at dinner time for dessert. Grandpa was good at getting me started on thinking outside the box. He gave me a book of planets to study at about age 5. My Grandma O. was interested in people's health all her life. In her early days, she had hoped to become a doctor but got a degree in nursing. I remember her sitting in the hospital room quietly while I was seriously ill with a groin gland infection and a high fever. She sat beside me like a guardian angel. I felt loved by her and very much comforted by her presence. When I got home, my dad would carry me up and down the stairs when I needed to go to the bathroom. Before long, I recovered and was back to my usual self.

My dad would let me comb his hair and make little ponytails a few times. He was a handsome man with wavy black hair. He shaved every day.

One day at the dinner table (age 5), I declared, "Dad is the smartest man in the world." Mom and Dad let out a surprised chuckle and smiled at my profound statement.

Every day we would run over next door to Grandma and Grandpa H's little house. Grandma would let us grandkids play in her flour and sugar bin when mixing some bread or cookies. She was a fun-loving, sensible grandma. I recall that she chased us (grandkids) around the dining table when occasionally baby-sitting. Sometimes we would join her as she tried to nap in her bed, but we kept her awake with our constant movements. When she took care of us in the evening, she would come and rest with me on my queen bed in the big farmhouse while my parents went out.

As I grew up, I was free-spirited and happy-go-lucky. When I was old enough to start school, I told Grandpa that the bus did not need to pick me up. I loved being at home. I had lots of fun there. I did not see any reason to change things by attending school. Grandpa would often laugh about the many things I would say. Grandpa let me speak my mind. His laughter made me happy.

Elementary school was not the place that I wanted to be. Our music teacher often chose me to play musical parts on stage. But I found one way or another to get out of it by "being sick." Reading was difficult, and I was not interested in anything but playing and exploring at home. The comics section of the newspaper interested me the most. A schoolteacher ordered a book for me as motivation, but I wouldn't say I liked to read.

Age 6

For a short while longer, I had Snowby as a companion. Sadly, we lost her to heartworm. I learned early in life about the sorrows of losing a close, trusted companion and an immediate family member. I also lost my Grandma O. from a heart attack around this time.

When the weather was nice, I learned to ride Mom's 26-inch adult bike. She had me practice on the grass, I stood on the peddles, and the seat was too high to sit on. Also, I begged my mom for a toy sewing machine at this age, and she decided to let me use hers. I read pictures on the pattern instructions rather than reading the words when sewing clothes.

As a child, I would dig for worms and climb a prickly evergreen tree to feed the baby Robins. It was fascinating to see their beaks wide open, ready for a worm! I loved learning about nature and being out in it very much.

We had an elm tree in our yard that Dad turned into a treehouse. There was another tree near Grandma and Grandpa's house that my Uncle Ted, their son, used a tractor to tie the swing. It may have been more than 12 feet from the ground. It was an exceptionally long ride back and forth. When we closed our eyes on the swing, it would tickle our tummies. Uncle Ted was full of fun and humor, unlike his older brother, my dad.

Dad loved to watch the black and white T.V. that Mom won by counting freckles on a face in the local newspaper. But she wanted to enjoy some conversation, regretting that we had ever gotten it in 1967. We loved watching I Love Lucy, My Three Sons, Leave it to Beaver, Petticoat Junction, Green Acres, and many more shows. Dad and Mom loved to watch Lawrence Welk.

While sitting around the dining table, I always had many sad and angry feelings toward my dad and longed to express myself. He mostly ignored us kids, although my sister was his favorite.

Age 7

I told my mom my plans to go to college one day. "Without knowledge, you can't go to college," I declared. Mom agreed, 'Yes, that is right." She replied. Mom nearly always agreed with whatever I said. She encouraged me to be creative, which was highly acceptable in our family. Her sister (my aunt) was inspired to succeed and flourish with her parents (my grandparents) encouragement. She drew her art in fashion merchandising and advertising for media outlets in New York City during the 1950s. She got her art degree from the Minneapolis College of Art and Design.

During wintertime, my energetic Grandma H., while in her seventies, took us sledding down Hanson's Hill! My grandpa and grandma H. lived on the farm next door in a smaller, newer house. She loved going for long walks, no matter what season it was. She grew yellow and orange tulips every spring on the east side in front of her little two-bedroom house.

Once I said to her while we were playing in the woods, "Grandma, do you wish you were young again? "

"Yes!" She smiled as she imagined herself young too.

She loved to watch Daniel Boone on her black-and-white T.V.

When we took outdoor walks, Grandma H. would explain the trees and plants names. She and Grandpa had more than 20 fruit trees in the orchard, mostly apples: Winesap, Whitney, MacIntosh, Honey Gold, Granny Smith, Delicious, Honeycrisp, and one we called a School Apple because it was ready to eat by the time school began in the fall. The farm's orchard had Gooseberry Bushes, Plum trees, Concord Grape Vines, Pear Trees, and huge extra-large Raspberries in Grandma's and Grandpa's Garden. We happily helped ourselves to the berry patch. My sister, brother, and I spent endless summer hours in the apple trees eating green apples. The orchard was our paradise!

Toady and I would play with the mice in the empty corn crib. We would catch them by their tails. They would try to bite us. We also played with the cats and kittens in an enormous farm barn in the haymow. We were happy!

Often on winter Sunday afternoons, Mom would make us hot chocolate with a marshmallow floating on the top in her coffee cups. We would play Yahoo, Crazy Eights, Chinese Checkers, and Monopoly. I made myself the creative Monopoly Banker who managed the money. That was not how you played the game. My younger siblings often went along with it, and my parents ignored how I changed game rules. We played Chutes and Ladders during our early years, and later we played the Game of Life.

Age 10

Occasionally Grandma H. and I would have disagreements. One time, she worried that a chain letter she had gotten would bring bad things to her if she did not forward it. I reassured my worried Grandma that she would be fine if she ignored that letter. Grandma corrected my English as I spoke and taught me a few German words. When she was in her twenties, she taught in a country school. Grandma also helped me with my Sunday School lessons when I was a young teenager. She fed me her wholesome, tasty, one-of-a-kind oatmeal cookies at snack time.

I dawdled on the piano and created a few songs that Mom thought were great. She brought me to my lessons for several years, but I was never serious about playing. She also got me started on a clarinet when I was in fifth grade. Aunt Ginny used to have an antique solid silver one. My sister got a clarinet too. We both wanted a flute far more than the clarinet.

I had an interest in writing books. "Jenny's Pets" was the first story I wrote. I made the cover from cardboard, drew pictures, and wrote the letters by hand with a pencil. At that point in time, I couldn't understand how book writers knew how many pages to put into a book. I had extra blank pages even after the story was complete. Also, I wrote a book called "Nibbles Finds a Mate." A rabbit love story. Blue construction paper for the cover. Then, I created the title and drew the art with crayons. My close aunties and uncles on my mom's side gave me praise. I dedicated the stories to them. Thinking and writing were my safe ways to express myself since dad didn't want to hear me say anything.

I found many beautiful rocks when walking around the farm. I collected some in a box, then stored them in the haymow.

Grandpa and Dad made us a rolling teeter-totter out of metal wheels attached to the axis. The board balancing on the axis was painted dark green, and there were metal handles on both ends of the board. We rolled around the yard and teetered up and down. Everyone loved getting their chance to ride it.

More Random Memories

My neighbor's cousins would come over on Halloween to trick or treat. I thought I could safely trick them with washed-up soup bones in a wrapper one year. It was a surprising trick that did not hurt anyone. They did not bother to stop at our house anymore on Halloween.

My mom loved chickens. Every spring, she would order chicks from Murray McMurray Hatchery in Webster City, Iowa. She would get a wide variety, including interesting ones like Buff Laced Polish with top hats on their heads and Araucana Chickens that laid green eggs. We also had many more pretty-colored chickens and Brahmas with feathers that grew on their legs and feet; they laid Brown eggs. Turkens had no feathers on their necks.

We ate the Broiler Chickens that my mom raised. Broilers are thick, meaty chicken. Dad and Grandpa raised feeder cattle. We had excellent cuts of beef to eat. We also harvested potatoes and vegetables and stored them in the freezer or the cool room in the basement. The cool room had an unforgettable earthy smell to it.

Every week Mom made bread from scratch. She wrote a note, "The Queen of Hearts, she made some tarts, have one." We got a kick out of that!

Grandma loved to raise a big garden of vegetables. She was

generous in sharing her harvest with relatives and neighbors.

My parents also had a lovely one-acre garden. They grew sweet corn, acorn squash, green and purple beans, tomatoes, sweet peas, carrots, and radishes. My aunt would often harvest the extra beans for her seven children.

My Grandpa H. was a happy and kind man, for which I am grateful. He allowed me to be with him while working around the farm. I helped him plant and harvest potatoes, feed the cattle, watch him butcher chickens, and help stack bales and paint farm buildings. I will always appreciate that my grandparents included me in day-to-day farm activities. I thought my Grandpa H. was a brilliant man—but- he only had an eighth-grade education. He was exceptionally sharp when it came to cattle markets and farming. Grandpa lived to be 97. His brother, also our neighbor, made it to 100. Another brother, who lived in rural Bemidji, Minnesota, probably would have lived that long if a barn he was trying to save did not fall on him in his eighties.

Age 11

Around Christmas, I saw some beautiful, colorful ties in my little brother's closet. One long necktie had a pretty peacock on it. Another was bright yellow with sunshine and flowers, and there were even more brilliant colorful ties. I thought they would make an excellent gift for Dad. I wrapped them up and put them under the tree. My dad opened the present and smiled slightly without saying anything. Mom got a kick out of the gesture, chuckled, and remarked about forgetting he had those colorful ties.

Age 12

One time for my dad's birthday, I wrote on a card, "I love you!" Dad responded angrily, "Well, why don't you show it!" I gave up giving him a birthday card until many decades later. I wanted to carry on a conversation with him, but he did not want to talk about anything with me. There were times that he would say I was good for nothing. He would often say that I was never going to amount to anything. Usually, I cried at the dining table. I accidentally spilled milk or food or dropped silverware or dishes a few times. Dad was sure to scold me. Life with him was miserable.

My happiest moments were mainly outside on the farm or spending time with grandma, grandpa, and cousins! Sometimes I would walk the dusty gravel roads with dogs that people would rehome or abandon at our farm. Many kitties came to us also.

A sack swing hung from a limb about eight feet from the ground. I spent hours tossing the sack swing up into the tree where it hung. I scurried up the tree, standing on the branch from which the sack swing was hanging, put the sack between my legs, and then jumped off the limb. I repeatedly enjoyed a big thrill every time! I was skinny, around 98 pounds, and energetic.

I found an old wire mattress in the woods. I turned it into a trampoline by weaving Jute bale twine over and under the wires. Then I set the homemade trampoline up on oil barrels. We joyfully jumped for hours and hours! I had the most fun using my innovative energy to make things. My siblings, cousins, and I had many enjoyable days with that creation of mine.

Teen Years

In the late evenings, I would climb up the side of the granary barn in Winter, where grandpa and dad stored field corn. Then I landed on the top of the short calf barn. I laid down on the snow-covered roof. For many hours over the years, I looked up at billions and trillions of brilliant, beautiful stars any day of the year. There I felt close to my Creator.

Having grandparents next door meant that we would often see our many cousins. We played outdoor games like kickball, croquet, hide and seek, and touch tag. You name it! There were barn lofts to scale into, barn doors to climb on to the rooftop, apple trees to scramble into, apples to eat, raspberry patches to graze from, and farm animals to play with, including kittens, calves, and chicks. I made friends with many of the critters and spent hours with them. I tamed a few calves, especially one that I named Violet. I gave Violet many hugs around her neck and talked about whatever I had on my mind. For such a giant cow, she was pretty gentle. Tame cows made the milking process easier for my dad.

My sister had one favorite calf that she called Petunia. The whole family fed, watered, and cared for all the animals. We shoveled cow droppings out of the barn, and I usually washed the milking deck with a spray hose. Life on the farm was delightful! I am forever grateful for that experience.

My parents encouraged my sister to learn how to drive the tractor. Everyone in the family would say how much she looked like her father. My dad wanted a boy in the family. She was the favorite and got praised for helping around the farm. Dad got a Skid Steer to use for chores as time went on. It fascinated me. I did not bother to ask to use it. I hopped on, buckled up, and moved around anything I wanted. It was small and easy to run. However, Dad and Grandpa let me know that I should be in the house cleaning, sewing, and cooking. I did not take their suggestions seriously. They did not stop my determination to drive the Skid Steer. Dad should have taken advantage of my ambition and given me regular jobs around the farm. I loved being outdoors! My sister and I weren't afraid to get our hands dirty. We dug into whatever task was before us. Every spring, we helped pick up rocks in the fields, a very consuming, muscle-building task.

Grandma played an essential role in studying the Bible. She wanted us to know all the stories. Her daughter (my aunt) taught Psalms and Proverbs. Speed Reading was another class she taught at the Oak Hills Bible Institute. I was never a speed reader, but I did enjoy the many stories of the Old Testament and the stories of Jesus. My aunt was a director at the local camps during the summers. I learned something about public speaking from her since she gave many talks at area churches around Minnesota. She had attended Moody Bible Institute after high school. Grandma and Grandpa's 3rd son (my uncle) was a preacher. He was mentally gifted, as shown by his high grades in college. His sermons were boring and complicated to follow.

When Grandpa, Dad, and other neighboring relatives worked in the field, grandma would make a massive lemonade container to take them, along with homemade cookies and sandwiches.

Nothing could replace my love for the outdoors. Mom knew how much I wished for a horse, and much to my dad's dismay, she got me one that I named Bess, a Welsh-Quarter Horse mix. In eighth grade, here is the Haiku poem that I wrote:

"To feel a horse's soft, fuzzy nose is like velvet; you will like it!"

The horse was pregnant with a foal; my dad was extremely unhappy with the extra two mouths to feed. When the beautiful colt was born, I was so excited! I watched them out in the yard in the cold spring rain. Not long after, the colt died. The mother horse was unsettled for several months after that. As usual, I rode her without a saddle one hot summer day. She took off galloping. By the time she stopped, I was hanging upside down on her neck. Mom decided to trade her for a miniature Shetland Pony. Shetland horses are known to be stubborn about moving, but not Silkie. She galloped! One day I had a painful landing! Thud! My tail bone hit hard cement. Then a neighbor offered to buy Silkie from Dad for $20 for his youngest daughter. My dad happily got rid of the horse. Mom tried to get Silkie back from the neighbor. The neighbor told her to get off his property, or he would shoot her. That was the end of any more horses.

We stayed busy with many kinds of farm work and jobs. Neighboring families often called me to babysit, but soon I let my sister take most of those jobs. One summer, my sister and I "walked soybeans." We hand-weeded and hoed several acres of them. We both got badly sunburned! That burn mark stayed with me for years. I also walked a few neighbors' soybeans and, one time, I got severely dehydrated.

Sometimes I answered phone calls from local farmers regarding their cows' artificial insemination requests. They would let me know which bull they wanted to breed their cows. Then I would write down the information for the breeder.

My upbringing was wholesome and enjoyable in most ways. I learned to value hard work and the sense of teamwork required for a farm to be successful. Most of our immediate family and extended families were close. We worked together like a reliable, dependable team.

While in high school, I took more math classes since my

favorite teacher, Mrs. Johnson, taught those classes., She taught basic math to me in 8th grade and other students with learning difficulties. I got a D minus in 7th-grade math with Mr. Carda. In 9th grade, I could choose between study hall with Mr. Carda or Algebra with Mrs. Johnson. I longed to be with the fun-loving gift of gab, Mrs. Johnson! During class, she would tell stories. She could talk easily for almost one hour straight. She made my day every time we students went to her class. I took additional math classes to avoid study hall and stay with my favorite math teachers. Mr. Sailer came after Mrs. Johnson retired. It was good for me to build my brain! I tried new student activities like choir and volleyball also.

I lost my Grandma H. from liver cancer when I was 14. My boyfriend, a chiropractor, believed those yellow toxic pest strips used in her kitchen might have caused cancer.

In 9th grade, I joined the marching band. We worked hard and endured hot, muggy summertime practices and parades in heavy wool uniforms with unbreathable hats. I experienced dehydration during some of those parades. My band members and I would get drenched in embarrassing sweat.

I got my very first swat on the butt from my father at age 15 while I was doing the dishes. I was incredibly shocked and extremely puzzled why that suddenly happened. There would be no fun around him. It puzzled me why I couldn't figure out why he was so glum all the time. He never hugged me. He was cold and uncaring, never giving me positive attention. The negativity was bothersome to me. It's not what I wanted in a father. Mom was lucky to have the dad she had. He was affectionate and caring towards her. Grandpa O. and Grandpa H. were very good to me. I was grateful for both grandpas.

The Farmer's Almanac had published an informative food chart about the vitamins and minerals in certain foods and the diseases caused by the lack of that food. I saved that magazine and took the information to heart. I later applied the learned knowledge to a chicken with paralysis. Mom separated the ailing chicken into an unoccupied farm building. I reasoned from the chart that the chicken could probably use the minerals found in cow's milk. I gave the chicken some milk to drink. In about 24 to 36 hours, her paralysis disappeared. She was walking normally! Mom was in awe over the two-and-two I put together. She thought her teen daughter solving that problem was brilliant! She bragged about me. I expected that!

In my senior year, I wandered casually by the house after chores. I caught mom gazing happily and lovingly at my senior year picture when I looked through the porch window. I never told her that I saw her through the windows. She loved her favorite picture of me. I loved another favorite twelfth-grade picture of me. I managed to be overly vain about myself.

"Wildfire', a song about a pony, was one of my favorite songs during my high school years.

One day I took a picture of Dad taking his noon nap in his comfortable chair with a long-haired, mixed-breed Norwegian Forest cat in his lap. I treasured that picture!

Around the farmyard, we often saw a barn cat casually walking across the gravel – a barn swallow would chirp and dive in loops above the cat. It was a familiar summer scene. Mom would exclaim every time the wren would sing its familiar song around the Walnut tree on the east side of our big house, "Oh! I love my little wrenny!"

I've had the privilege to see hundreds of Monarch Butterflies gathered around Honey Suckle Bushes on the north side of the farm. I could not get enough of nature!

When I learned how to drive a car, I decided to give some people extra tomatoes in a neighboring small town. It was a tremendous donating experience for me, as the residents were appreciative.

One day dad gave me a teaching moment. "The wife does nice things for her husband." I glanced at him and made a face since he wasn't looking at me. It didn't matter what I thought anyway.

I still have fond summer memories of my dad and grandpa moving hay bales into the big red barn. Dad stomped on the giant hooks with his ankle-laced brown leather boots. Rectangular bales (a group of around 8 or 9 small bales) went up into the barn at a time. My grandpa drove forward, connected to the pulley and pins with a tractor. I watched in amusement as the bales stopped at the top of the entryway into the barn. Grandpa waited on the tractor for Dad to yell, "OK!" Then Grandpa would drive the tractor forward slowly. All the bales would make it into the barn most of the time. Rarely did one break apart on the way up. When the hooks came back empty, it looked like a colossal-sized spider coming out of the top of the barn.

I habitually came in especially late for supper to avoid my father at the table. He had it in his mind that I was rebellious. Truthfully, I was a very obedient teenager that rarely got into trouble while out with my high school friends. My grandmother was a longtime friend of neighbors about almost 3 miles away. Their daughter Susan was the leader of our high school click of 6 girls. Most of us were not troublemakers. We were A and B Honor Students. One evening we went into Juba's grocery store in Pipestone to pick up some things. Susan fun-lovingly grabbed an older man's grocery list and helped him shop for items on the list. He was good-natured, and he said it made his day.

Another time, we drove around Worthington and went into a couple of different bars. A man offered Susan a drink which she accepted. When we left the bar, Susan was our driver. She backed into a car, then quickly sped off. Soon we were going over the speed limit, and someone who was probably at the bar chased us in their car. We were terrified! I wasn't sure if we would come out of the situation alive! It was a terrifying ride back home! When I arrived home after 1 a.m., Mom was quite angry. I was not in control of what happened. It was hard to explain to her since she wouldn't hear the details. I decided never to go on a drive with Susan again.

All in all, I'm grateful for my childhood and everything my parents and grandparents taught me. Yet, even with this enjoyable start in life, I was still not entirely prepared for the chaos I would face in my future.

CHAPTER 2
College Years

Junior College

Before I graduated from high school in May 1977, I enrolled in Bethany Junior College in Mankato, Minnesota. My family dropped me off at the campus to begin my new academic life. We were all in tears except Mom. She seemed ready to accept that I was leaving home since I would be making college my future. After settling in, I cried for days since I was homesick for my family, friends, and the life I once knew. Within a few days, I quickly made new friends. I went home almost every weekend to Southwest Minnesota. It was awesome to get back home and catch up with loved ones.

I met a young lady that got rejected by her assigned roommates. Then we became roommates. I urged her to take showers and maintain good hygiene. I overdid showers – taking two per day. I was obsessed with avoiding germs. Chris and I got used to each other. After that, I began to understand how to deal with people who seemed different from me.

For my classes, I only wanted brand-new textbooks, nothing old. I also needed brand new clothes to wear and Mary Kay Cosmetics. I was tall, very lean, and overly vain! I wasn't too serious about school and enjoyed all the entertaining people around me. I mostly laughed and found lighthearted fun wherever I went.

I didn't get into trouble at all! I wrote a few Bible verses and hung them in classrooms and dining halls. It was a Bible school which made it okay. The tall, dark-haired student pastor that was my crush snarled repulsively and didn't like what I hung up in the dining hall. He ripped the signs wildly off the door a few feet ahead of me! I laugh out loud about it now!

A senior classmate (whose dad was the Dean of the college and a pastor) teased me quite a bit and called me a "whipper-snapper." I mostly avoided him. Sammy would not win my affection this way. He would try to have a conversation with me, but I would say "Hi" without stopping to talk with him. My room-mate Chris would smile big and often laugh whenever Sammy came around. She became obsessed with him, writing countless love letters. Eventually, Chris asked a college professor to find out if he was interested in her from the young man. The answer came back "no," he was not interested in her.

One of my favorite memories at Bethany was the chance to play the pipe organ in the chapel. I played hymns for fun for many days and hours without end. The daily chapel was for all students. Many students studying the pipe organ had lessons and practice times here and there throughout the days of the week, so I didn't play it then. I felt so much happiness playing those ancient songs from hymn books that were no longer used by some of the local churches back home that mom had gotten at some point. Music was my therapy. Once, the organ teacher came out from her nearby office to chat with me. I wasn't her student, but she knew I thoroughly enjoyed the old hymns that reminded me of family and home. She kindly told me to be aware that her students needed their practice. She knew that I enjoyed the beautiful sounds so much, so she let me continue playing. When student visitors came to the school, I played several old hymns. A high school-aged young man stood with the chapel door open, just listening for a while. I had turned my head to discover his interest, but the music was so enjoyable that I continued to play to my heart's content. I didn't notice when he left the chapel. Then, as usual, I played more hymns. I slowly got used to being less homesick as the weeks passed.

Time went by, but college wasn't going as well as I had hoped. I had trouble concentrating on complex subjects like Chemistry and many other challenging courses related to reading. Instead, I was interested in my Gymnastics, Basketball, Roller Skating, and Square-Dancing classes. Physical activities grabbed my interest! I enjoyed moving around and found it impossible to sit still and listen to lectures for long periods. I was pretty good at making close friends. I was friendly and curious about what my classmates were interested in doing. We would talk for hours about anything you could imagine. Like most teens, I frequently daydreamed about the attractive young men on campus. By this time in my life, my hair was a gold color when in the bright sunshine. I often had conversations with other girls about the guys they wanted to spend time getting to know. I had a massive crush on a dark-haired, handsome, tall guy named Greg. He did not seem to be interested in me at all! He eventually became a pastor.

Art and Lola were an older couple that we got to know. They lived directly across the dead-end street from the Chapel Pastor's son. Chris had a severe crush on Sammy. We usually went to Art and Lola's house about once or twice a week and had beautiful conversations about various topics. We heard their life stories. Art was blind, so Chris and I walked on each side of him to the

Chapel service every Wednesday evening, having enjoyable conversations as we walked the road. Lola worked at the college cafeteria. She cooked excellent meals that she shared with us; it was almost like a taste of home when she invited us for dinner.

My roommate graduated from college in the spring. I stayed at the dormitory a few days longer to volunteer for Minnesota Citizens Concerned for Life. I gathered survey information from local people. This organization was meaningful to me. I wanted to support their mission however I could. Volunteer work was interesting since I talked to many people with different opinions and ideas. It helped me to think more broadly and deeply.

Then I went home for the summer. I started sewing at Pipestone Manufacturing. I sewed pocket flaps all day long. One day at work, a wholly sewn orange and black plaid flannel jacket caught my eye. I knew I had to buy it for Grandpa!

"Great work, Aren," he grinned, "You did a nice job!" he exclaimed. Grandpa made me feel special. I was grateful!

A couple of months later, the company relocated to South Dakota. After that, I started working at the local meat center. My job was severely exhausting, lifting prime, choice, and ground beef and cleaning up around the place, so I was often tired. It was a four-day week, with Wednesdays off. My mom's cousin's husband was a State Meat Inspector. He encouraged me to avoid a life-long career working at that company due to the job's heavy demands and lack of advancement opportunities. I knew I wasn't going to stay.

Most of our family has always been very close. Being away from home at college did not change that. I always looked forward to seeing my many cousins, aunts, and uncles when I came home for visits during the summer or semester breaks. My dear paternal grandfather always sent me away to college with a package of creamed oatmeal cookies. I loved spending time just being with him. He was an excellent father and a grandfather combined into one fantastic individual! I could talk to Grandpa H. about almost anything. I had to speak my loudest since he was hard of hearing. It took some effort to raise my voice since I was trained to be quiet by his son. Grandpa had a friendly, cheery disposition, while my father was mainly grouchy. We smiled and enjoyed talking about family members and what they were planning and doing while sitting together in the kitchen or living room. He also watched television or listened to pop music and the news on the radio. We also worked outside on farm chores together.

Four-Year College (South Dakota State University)

I started classes at South Dakota State University in the fall of 1979. I was admitted on academic probation because my G. P. A. from junior college was below 2.0. I registered for three classes. I worked super hard to get the best grades possible. I succeeded. I got C's in Sociology and Chemistry and an A in Algebra. My grade point average increased ever so slightly. Then, I went to a counselor for advice on what courses I should sign up for compared to an aptitude test that I was given. I am visually oriented, which represents a learning style of its own. I decided to take art classes. I knew I would enjoy this creative adventure. I began to have the most fabulous time at college now. Here I found my place. One day in Fabric Design class, I hung up a brown 100% cotton fabric for a joke that I experimented with by folding it a few times and then placing it in a bit of bleach. The bleach ate a hole in the material. Dr. Helen Morgan surprised me by submitting my artwork to the student art gallery.

I frequently visited the South Dakota Art Museum to view new artists' work. I regularly viewed Harvey Dunn Paintings, Marghab Linens, Native Dakota Costumes, and Jewelry.

Dr. Norman Gambill taught Art History there with great passion. One day in person, I explained that the classroom's humidity made me sleepy. After that, he surprised his students with an occasional emphasis on words to wake us up. I proudly and diligently worked hard on memorizing exciting facts about ancient art. The tests were in essay form. I finally saw results from commitment and perseverance. I got an A.

I would often be the only one working in some art classes alone during the night and on the weekends. I was intrigued by creating works of art. One of my Elephant Ears Plant pencil drawings was on display at an Interior Design Show at the college, which made me very proud! Someone else loved it, too, and it disappeared – stolen! I mentioned it was missing, but the people I talked to couldn't tell me where it went. I couldn't believe it!

The following semester I registered for a drapery-making class where I met an Interior Design instructor who encouraged me to get into the Home Economics major. Then, I signed up for weaving, drawing, and fabric design art classes. I failed a merchandising class miserably.

While in college, I didn't spend much extra time with boyfriends, only in public spaces. I worked in the college cafeteria. I was happy to create art for hours and hours and listen to the radio. Studying was difficult. I had a hard time concentrating on words in textbooks. My smart boyfriend from India offered to help me learn. I really should have taken him up on his offer. He was brilliant, and I enjoyed listening to him say what he had to talk about with his adorable accent. He kept getting only A grades in all his classes. Phi Kappa Phi was disappointingly out of reach for me. There are very gifted people in this world. I can be the best me there is! The classes where I could use my creativity were the only classes I could get an A!

The summer at home when I turned 21 was very tough with my father. He took his anger out on me. Mom, dad, and I were in the kitchen. I can't remember what I did to make him angry at me. I remember his red, ugly, angry face snarling at me, grabbing and twisting my left breast, pushing me down to the floor, and getting on top of me. I clawed at his face in my defense mode. He wore that injury to church and wherever he went. I was grateful that mom had gotten him up and off me. I wanted to die. I ran out of the house, went to the woods, and lay down under an evergreen tree. I decided that I would not eat anymore. After a couple of days, I broke that way of dying promise to myself. I was very depressed. It was good that I sought a counselor for "talk therapy." I even had trouble explaining to my therapist what happened because I felt so much sadness and shame that the bad event happened with my father. I preferred being away and out of his presence more than ever before. I was severely depressed and eventually determined to continue my life.

I was involved with the Campus Crusade for Christ. Several of us met with our Bible study leader, who was in the military reserves while studying at SDSU. It was a sort of dating service and socializing event for many of us students. On spring break in March, we went to Daytona Beach, Florida. I volunteered to let the group use my new Chevrolet Chevette to drive from South Dakota to Florida. Our group took two cars to meet for the national Campus Crusade for Christ Convention. As usual,

I called mom to tell her about my plans to go to the convention. In the background, I could hear dad yell, "You can't go!" Mom didn't discourage my adventuresome idea whatsoever. I knew it was the right thing to do. Having FUN was what I was going to have! I met many other young men and women from many different colleges, and we attended workshops on how to live our lives as believers in Christian values. We also attempted to do some "witnessing" on the beach. I did not shine so well in witnessing. I didn't care to force my beliefs onto others, and I'm still that way. I enjoy discussions about God, Jesus, and the Holy Spirit, but only if people want to talk about spiritual matters.

One great experience to never forget was the chance to join the Pride of the Dakotas SDSU Marching Band. Dr. Walker directed the band. Fred was our Drum Major. We marched down Pennsylvania Avenue for President Ronald Reagan's Inaugural Parade. A college choir director and I filled in the Tuba section - not for sound but physically. I accepted this adventure with no questions because I have always enjoyed trying new things and being open to new experiences.

I covered my sandals with black socks for the Hobo Parade and marched with the "Pride" around our campus town. I don't think anyone noticed my feet! I would occasionally run into Dr. Walker on the college campus. He would ask me, "How's my favorite band member?" I would smile and reply, "Great!" After the Inaugural parade, I took lessons to play the flute because I had always wanted to learn this unique musical instrument.

At this university, I met students from all over the country and in many parts of the world. As I began making new friendships and exploring romantic interests, some of my boyfriends were foreigners. The first one came from Kenya. The next, from

India, was a Phi Kappa Phi member. I fell in love, but getting emotionally close to him wasn't easy. Being a strong student, he couldn't understand why I was having such trouble with school. I still did admire his brainpower and the goals for achieving in his life. He worked with ease on a master's degree in Civil Engineering. It amazed me that one could get straight A's through college! To top it off, he was model-type stunning—a typical 6-foot tall, dark, and handsome.

I went to conventions and field trips with other American Society of Interior Design Students. One was in Chicago. We enjoyed the view from the top of the Sears Tower and went for a walk around downtown Chicago after dark. My father scolded me about our not playing it safe. Thankfully there were more than a dozen of us! It was an unforgettable experience hearing the streetwalkers and drug dealers yelling at the street corners. That trip rounded my perception of human nature and lifestyles beyond my rural upbringing. I was grateful to experience more of the world, which helped me become a more culturally aware and understanding person.

In one incident, a fun-loving prankster at the college called my phone one day to say that band members had to get dressed up and be ready at half-time for the football game. I dressed in the band uniform and carried a large white tuba to meet the other band members. I found no one there. "Oh, LOOK!" I heard someone in the bleachers yell. I was way more amused than embarrassed by who the prankster was. I felt out of place, for sure! I smiled a little. I was a good sport and didn't know who thought of such a creative, harmless prank to this day!

Another time I saw that a harmless prankster had hoisted my parked car tire way up on top of the sidewalk. I laughed out loud over that surprise!

I did not discuss my struggles with classes as far as my studies went. That was tough for me to get right. I was not good at answering test questions and often amused my instructors and other students with my crazy essay answers. On a positive note, I had proven to myself more than a handful of times that I could skip the rough draft of research papers to submit a completed report by shuffling opened books around and writing from memory while preparing the paper. If there ever was an expert at procrastinating and cramming, it was me! I waited for nearly the last minute on everything! I'd go to class. After class, I'd go back to my dormitory room to finish typing and go to the office to turn the paper in to Mrs. Yost. I got a few points taken off and still got 90% plus grades on my research papers. Mrs. Yost directed us to put our citations on the same page as the topic we discussed in our papers. She liked how I followed her directions compared to other students who left all sources until the end of their papers.

One day in class, Mrs. Yost and the Dean of the Home Economics Department, Dr. Esee at SDSU, openly exposed my many low grades to the rest of the students. Some were protective of me, but others were shocked. The truth was out, and I was incredibly embarrassed! I also couldn't understand why it was necessary to expose my struggles. Oh well! The cat was out of the bag now! What were my teachers trying to do to me?

I received an Outstanding Interior Design Student Award voted by my classmates, not because of my grades but because I often participated in classroom discussions, worked diligently on my assignments wents, and interacted with the other students. They noted that I took my attendance seriously. Another student received an award based on her academic excellence, and I was in awe of her - she was indeed bright. Students discussed whether she should receive a recognition award, and she snapped at them and defended her right to be honored. I would have supported that right, too, if I had been deserving. I was very relieved that she could have her award. I secretly enjoyed my popularity vote. Besides learning about interior design, I also learned about friendships, social skills, and academic life.

At SDSU, I made many new friends. Often, I spent time with students in church activities. I was a church hopper and visited many. At one church, I heard the bell choir perform, and after the service, I asked the choir director how one could try out for the chorus. The bell choir director said I could come to the weekly practice to play music with them. What a tremendous opportunity! I was living the dream! I LOVED the sound! Working with others to make beautiful music was truly rewarding and like a miracle. It took teamwork. I loved playing bells so much that I even played solos, one bell at a time. I spent hours and hours making music. One day I was encouraged to accompany my handbell director on the organ, and my family came to see me play a few melodies. I was so happy to share my beautiful music!

I spent endless creative hours in the art classes I loved so much! Then, I worked in the college cafeteria and spent a little of my time with whatever foreign boyfriend interested me. My friend from India and I would drive in his green car, hang out with friends, go to a restaurant, see a movie, or walk around the campus.

When Mr. Handsome India finished his master's degree, I helped decorate a restaurant's basement for his graduation party with balloons and a banner that screamed "CONGRATULA-TIONS!" He greatly surprised me with an enthusiastic painful punch in my stomach during the gathering! So even though I had a massive crush on him, I couldn't get attached to him. I continued to enjoy learning about his life and culture. We spent hours working in the college cafeteria, studying at the library, and talking with friends. Occasionally in little spare time, we went roller skating.

It had taken me much longer than usual to get a diploma. I had to drop a few classes here and there because I was in danger of failing them. It became a habit, and I always wanted to take more art classes. I took many more art courses than my major required. Mom would firmly ask, "When are you going to be done?" I had no concrete answer.

I often had to say what she wanted to hear when it came to Mom instead of being truthful. I became good at lying about school and life, in general, to make her happy.

My grandpa, who followed my studies with interest, gave me a graduation present before I finished. Nobody else seemed to care about what I was doing on campus or why my education seemed to drag out.

Then I traveled out of state to participate in a professional practicum at an Arizona art gallery called the Small World Gallery. It was a fantastic opportunity where I learned much more about art and began to dream about a future doing the creative work I loved. However, I got homesick when I lived in an older couple's guest house when I went to Arizona. I also worked for temporary employment agencies while studying for school credit. At first, I cried at times while living there, but I soon got used to the dry, smoggy air and the new experience. I took the time to meet some second cousins. After that, I visited my second cousin in eastern Arizona. Then I traveled to see other relatives in Colorado Springs. I drove straight from Colorado Springs to Billings, Montana, for over ten hours straight, only stopping a couple of times at rest stops. I found a motel to go to sleep in for a few hours. Then, I went to Seattle to visit my friend Chris, my junior college roommate. By then, I was feeling brave and not homesick anymore.

The Small World Gallery owner taught me how to run an art gallery. I had the opportunity to do a professional practicum with her. I helped with the publicity of the many artists represented and learned all the details of managing the art gallery. After I finished the semester, I was amazed that Professor Yost gave me an A grade worth seven credits, which gave my G. P. A. a gigantic boost. I drove home to Southwest Minnesota and prepared to work in Minneapolis for the summer.

I often thanked my mom for getting me started with music in grade school while at South Dakota State University. I also called Mrs. Johnson several times to thank her for everything she did for me. I give her credit because she got me started in continuing higher math classes in high school and getting an A in Algebra at SDSU. Eventually, I earned a college diploma. I didn't participate in the graduation ceremony, but I sat with the rest of the audience and heard my name announced. My counselor made a curious comment on my decision: I didn't feel deserving of my diploma, and I had more learning to do for the rest of my life that lay beyond the classroom walls.

By December 1985, I had finished college and had not been back to visit the campus for almost 40 years. However, I still carry many memories about those early years when my life was developing intellectually, socially, and emotionally in ways that continued to impact me in the future.

CHAPTER 3
Choosing Mister Charming

After I graduated from SDSU with a degree, I decided to live in the basement of relatives in Windsor Heights, Iowa. My rent was $100 per month, and I went to work for temporary employment agencies until I found a position through an employment agency.

The mother/mother-in-law of a married couple referred me to the Finance Corporation they owned and ran. She made suggestions for office attire that I took to heart. I worked in their home office, answering the phone and calculating interest, among other odd jobs, including counting the number of printed cards from a printing company they hired. On weekends I worked for the Maintenance Department in Southridge Mall, cleaning windows and wiping tables in the food court.

At this point, my dating life became more active. I began seeing a young Scottish gentleman. He often smelled like alcohol, so I decided to break off the relationship. There were three young men I spent time with while working at the food court in the mall. One was a chain smoker and seemed quite lazy with tall questionable stories that he told me. I didn't want that one. Another young man said angry, hateful things about his dad, so I decided I didn't enjoy his companionship. Then along came Mr. Charming. While washing the windows, I noticed he saw me outside the arcade where he worked. Daniel was tall, about six feet two inches. His eyes were medium brown, and his hair was very curly. He was mainly cheerful and happy. I felt secure telling him honestly about my thoughts and feelings.

I drew a small house on the windowpane and wrote "Hi!" backward in the soap suds. We started talking, and we hit it off right away. Then we began spending quite a bit of time together.

After completing my weekend job, we decided to go to the weekend evening church services on Sundays. There, we watched Dr. James Dobson's "Strong-Willed Child" series. We also watched a pro-life movie about an unborn baby called "The Silent Scream."

Dan and I shared simple things like walking through the local Green Belt Park. We went to other area outdoor parks, also. We spent lots of time in the living room with his dad at his house. His younger brother would pace around the house nervously on shoes he bent the backs of into clogs. We often rode in the new gray Charger he had purchased after a bar owner's settlement. That came from an accident on his moped when a drunk driver struck him. It was good that he landed in the grass not far from a tombstone maker's business. Dan was unconscious in the hospital for a week. Following this period, I got to know him better after his recovery. He had a small hobby of raising hamsters in his dad's backyard shed.

Dan had lived downtown but moved back in with his dad when he discovered that inner-city areas could be especially crime-ridden. He lived with his dad and brother until we got married. He was 30, and I was 27.

I got to know about Dan's Hispanic heritage as well. In the

1800s, one of his ancestors, known to have blue eyes, came to the western hemisphere from the north of Spain - Basque country. These ancestors were shepherds. Since I am interested in generational history, I thought the information was intriguing!

The blue-eyed ancestor sailed to the Panamanian region in the mid-1800s and met a Central American native (of the Guna Tribe, formerly the Cuna people). This lady lived on the San Blas Islands.

Daniel's father got a scholarship to study at Drake University for Accounting. Then, he worked for over 30 years as a Times Analyst at John Deere. Daniel's father met his mother in Des Moines, Iowa, at a restaurant where she worked, and they eventually married. His mother had been previously married and had a daughter by her first marriage. The newlywed couple raised three sons, with Daniel in the middle. His mother faced a transverse birth with him. He was born on a sweltering hot day when the hospitals in the 1950s had no air conditioning.

His mother often played with the Ouija Board that spelled out, "Boy, go away! " He was the least favored son and was not always treated well. Dan was often sick with asthma and hyperactive. His parents' smoking worsened his asthma. One of the most incredible things he had going for him was having his grandma living with the family until he was in the eighth grade when she died. They enjoyed playing games together and cooking. He got along reasonably well with his father. However, his dad nicknamed him "Lilly" because he viewed his son as wimpy.

I thought well of his family. However, I think they teased Daniel too much on occasion, but he seemed to let it roll off his back. His father was very polite and respectful to me, and he thought Daniel got a real deal for a girlfriend when I came along. The older brother was a successful art teacher at a college in Michigan and played drums in a local band. In the late 1970s, he displayed a work of art at the Smithsonian.

Daniel tried junior college but was not successful. He worked part-time in a bank and an arcade. Dan believed his brothers were more successful in education and life than him, and I think he had low self-esteem. His artist brother described me as quiet and soft-spoken.

I felt accepted - very much so. Daniel's dad had great respect for women.

The family favorite was Jake, who was the baby brother. His much older half-sister had severe emotional problems, and Daniel felt some connection to her. When she was in the nursing home expecting to die of renal failure, he brought her a favorite McDonald's meal with fries before she passed away. He had previously taken care of his mother when he was a teenager, but she died when he was nineteen. Hearing these details, I felt like Dan had a good heart and would be a devoted family man.

When we met, my car was about ten years old, and I had a small bank account with a balance of less than $500, so extravagances were out of the question. We spent time with his friends, usually sharing a pizza and talking or watching television. We also found some hills in the neighborhood to sit on a skateboard and ride downhill. Sometimes we drove through downtown Des Moines, "scooping the loop" on a weekend night, listening to music on the car radio, and checking out other young people also out and about in our area. Sometimes we would drive out to the country to a beautiful place called "Sleepy Hollow." There was an old bridge over the Skunk River with many trees. Our dates were lighthearted and casual, which created a comfortable, meaningful relationship between us. There weren't any secrets or alarming observations to make me question anything.

Our conversations centered on the fact that he was looking for his Mrs. Charming. Acting on his plans, he proposed to me on three different occasions.

Ever since I was a child, I have wanted to get married and have a family. What I had seen in Daniel so far was encouraging. He was very respectful to his father, never arguing with him at any time, even when his father was upset by something Dan had done. Seemingly, we agreed on many things, including values and goals.

Daniel didn't have much interest in kissing. We held each other close and kept our clothes on. The relatives I stayed with did not think well of him; they had a daughter and a son. One time, Mr. Charming playfully grabbed Amy's baton from her and put the baton's ball in her crotch area. Looking back on life, what he did was a clear red flag.

Another time a "frenemy" who had tried to desert Daniel and drown him out in the country creek where they went for a drive. It was a place we called" Sleepy Hollow."

That "frenemy" once stated, "He likes them young."

"Young-looking," he had clarified. I thought the "frenemy" referred to me because, at age 23, college students and professors were sure I was 17. For a long time, I looked younger than my actual age.

As we continued to spend time together, I did not see any red flags to scare me away. We weren't getting any younger, and we both had jobs and were self-supporting. We remained close to our respective families. Our courtship continued for a year and a half. If I had any slight doubts, I pushed them away and focused on Dan's good qualities, telling myself everything was lining up for us to share a meaningful life looking forward.

After our marriage, Daniel and I moved to the Minneapolis area from Des Moines to find better jobs. The economy of the 1980s seemed to be better around larger cities, and we took regular weekend trips to Des Moines to see family and friends.

After we married, Daniel's feelings were more explosive. He got angry about something. I forgot what we were arguing about while living in our apartment. I went out for a drive, crying and talking to my Creator for comfort. He also threw our soft, prayer kneeling cushion at me in another incident while we were spatting. When he got angry, he grabbed my shirt collar and got into my face. Later he commented, "I won! " There would be other times throughout our marriage when we would get upset with each other over things he wrecked or whatever disagreement we had at the time. My family came over for a visit, and my brother-in-law recognized marijuana-smoking paraphernalia on the coffee table. My family was ready to help me go back home, but I was not eager to be in the downgrading presence of my father. I did not smoke. It was disappointing to realize that Daniel had not indeed quit the habit. He had lied to me about no more smoking. He was back to his addiction, forming another wedge between us. I was careful to avoid fighting flareups. I spent time away from the apartment more and more. He enjoyed watching television and playing videotapes. I joined a handbell group and spent time walking around local parks. We watched some television programs together. But something changed after we were married.

CHAPTER 4
It Was Love

Dan and I met at Southridge Mall. He worked in the arcade. Every weekend I cleaned the mall entry doors and windows and wiped off tables in the food court. He would walk into the food court to order some of his favorite foods. Dan was my crush! He saw me and wondered if I was the one! I felt the aura of his gentle, charming personality. Two or more months went by with occasional glances. During that time, I noticed his unique ears. I was attracted to him! I described them as unable to hold water if he stood on his head. My ears, like most people, have a folded flap on the outer top. His ears are slightly fanned out.

One day he was standing outside the arcade with bleeps and tones in the background with a slight potbelly, big shoes, an arcade vest, and those ears! And brown eyes that looked over at my wide-eyed, blue eyes.

I put soap on the door glass. I knew Dan was watching me, so I drew a house and wrote "Hi!" backward so he could read it. Then he came over to ask me if it was worth it to clean those windows since they'll get dirty again, and I said I was on the improvement committee.

One day there was an empty chair at the table he was sitting at in the food court. He let me know that he had reserved the seat for me. I was so very excited that I quickly sat down! Dan's sweet, gentle personality charmed me. He asked me if I had any boy-friends. I was so impressed with the courtesy and respect for other people and a current boyfriend I might have. I wasn't seeing anyone, I told him. While visiting Dan's family for some time, again and again, I saw the calm and respectful way he was with his dad when he yelled and screamed at Dan for loaning a friend some money.

We dated almost every day for over a year. We enjoyed each other's conversations and meals and went places in his new charger.

I let my personality go. My extreme mood swings were in the package. I gave Dan some of the most challenging times. Subconsciously I wanted to see if he could stand me for who I was. I hid nothing about my temperament. My love for a previous boy-friend faded very slowly. I often told Dan, "Maybe you love me more than I could ever love you." Driving home after one of our dates, he cried so much that he had to pull over to the side of the road. He proposed to me three times before I finally said "Yes." I was a terrified, nervous bride on our wedding day – hoping that this relationship would last forever.

The most significant difficulties were my intense mood swings, his messes around the house and yard, our ever-constant financial struggles, and a strong-willed toddler. It could have torn any relationship apart. We chose to love each other regard-less of circumstances, not basing our love only on feelings that come and go but loving each other unconditionally for who we are to each other. God has blessed me with you. I love you, Dan.

*He put the following note at the end of my "love memories story."

"I am your valentine. I always have been and always shall be yours. Dan."

Loving people unconditionally is only something Jesus Christ did best. I can't love unconditionally, I learned. I didn't even consider the thought of the abuse that was to come. It would have been a perfect love story, and Dan made some disastrous choices that would change everything!

CHAPTER 5
Our Family Ups & Downs

Despite the pain and desolation of confronting the fact of my children's abuse, I have one comfort. My two daughters had each other when they went through mistreatment from their father. If I had just one daughter, her isolation and suffering would have been difficult without someone to confide in who could understand the situation. Of course, I wish the girls had been able to tell me what was happening. But their father had threatened them with scary warnings about what would happen if they told anyone. They struggled to preserve our dysfunctional family by surrendering their right to report their father's misconduct to me or other authorities. They suffered in silence, but they had each other.

They were babies when the abuse began. They had no way to logically process what was happening to them or find a way to escape by leaving home or telling others what their father was doing. My husband put a wedge between our daughters and me by using fear to manipulate them. It worked. Young children can be frightened by the thought of hurting their loved ones. Their father told them our family would break up, and he would go to jail. Small children would never want to be responsible for sending their father to prison. That kind of power is horrifying to young children. I genuinely hate that they endured all that abuse from him in our home for many years. Thankfully, they are now free from ever having to see him again. They have learned the truth about what he did to them. They are continually healing from the emotional and psychological damage he caused.

The Homemade "WANTED" Poster
It was strange to see the peculiar poster my husband printed. He made several copies and scattered them around our city.

WANTED

NAME: Daniel Ross
D. O. B. X/X/XX
ALIASES: The Wanderer

Distinguishing Marks: Patch over left eye, tattoo on the left shoulder of a skull, and crossed bones.

Alleged Charges: Armed robbery, Assault, Assault with a deadly weapon, Assault of a police officer, unlawful flight, trafficking narcotics, attempted murder, robbery of a private citizen, inciting a riot.

Considered armed and dangerous. Take extreme caution. Claims to be a born-again Christian.

He used his driver's license for the picture and then drew a patch over his left eye and drew a beard and mustache. Ironically nearly 30 years later, he had an operation on that eye, and it's occasionally covered with a patch.

During the early 1990s, I built a family life centered on a household routine that seemed to work for everyone, based on the domestic training and family values I had learned from my parents and grandparents at home. I so much enjoyed raising my girls, cooking for them, shopping with them, and going home to visit my parents – their grandparents on the farm where I had grown up. I looked forward to its wholesome family environment to escape from our suburban home. I loved family life, especially with my daughters. I tried to get along with my husband as much as possible to keep our family together. But someone had to work to bring in income, which was mostly my responsibility. Dan also worked occasionally, despite growing health issues. While raising my daughters, I enjoyed taking them to many playgrounds and county and state parks.

One day there was light rain with no thunder or lightning. I parked the car. Out of the car, my girls jumped, running barefoot across the bright green grass drenched in fallen rainwater. I loved how free-spirited and carefree they were, laughing and happy. Sometimes we would go to the Cannon River Bridge Park to drop in rocks and leaves; then play at the playground with a tall metal slide.

I brought them to Walmart to buy nice, inexpensive clothes for them to wear and groceries. Our budget was tight, and I spent lots of time searching for clothes and household items at garage sales and thrift stores. While visiting Grandpa Ross one time in Des Moines, I splurged and bought two brand-new white satin dresses for the girls to wear. I took many pictures and treasured the moments.

In her early years, Tia went to church with me. She impressed the caregivers in the nursery, "She knows a lot!" one said. I smiled. "I read to her," I explained. Tia could count to 10 before she was one year old. At ten months, she would yell, "Daisy, Daisy!" to the neighbor's dog. Tia said "hi" and "okay" at three months old. She knew her alphabet by one and a half years old. I had the immense joy of holding her in my arms. I loved reading all kinds of educational and religious children's books. Occasionally when reading out loud, I would fall asleep. We snuggled together on the couch and watched an occasional TV program like Star Search and game shows. We sang children's songs together. When Tia was 18 months old, she would sing the whole song "Jesus Loves Me." Also, she could tell people her full name. At 22 months, she counted to ten after me when I counted ten scoops of chocolate Malt-O-Meal. Tia wanted to help with chores. She was around two years old when she tried to help me mow the grass in our yard with an antique reel mower that I picked up at the thrift store. Together we pushed the manual mower. She cried with determination to help me cut the grass. Tia, to this day, tries to help me with many tasks. We live together and help each other with the chores, maintaining our tiny two-bedroom house and growing gardens and flower plants on our small acreage.

She stated before age two, "Daddy's a man" (now that I look back, that is a red flag!) At 31 months, she said, "My name is Tia, Tia Woman" (that is also a red flag for me now!)

At Valley Fair in the summer of 1993, her favorite rides were: The Northern Lights (three times in a row), The Traveler, Super

Cat, The Octopus, and Tilt-A-Whirl. She had no fear on any of these rides, including the Scrambler.

One summer, we went to a cousin's wedding. My cousin's dad (Uncle Ted) took pictures of my mischievous four-year-old Tia running past my cousin's white, fluffy, long wedding dress and giving it a swat. Then Uncle Ted took a picture of Tia eating some wedding cake under the table. Uncle Ted was good at catching Tia having some mischievous fun! I treasure those fun-loving, carefree moments!

For fun, one day in the spring, when Tia was four and Ana was two; we watched a wedding dress pageant in a nearby town. Tia was absolutely thrilled to watch all the pretty dresses on beautiful models wearing them, and Ana enjoyed the display of white dresses all around us. It was a free wedding dress show, and that was what our budget allowed.

Difficult Times

Health issues played a role in our family struggles. Dan was diagnosed with Type 2 Diabetes just before the time our younger daughter Ana came along. He often had asthma attacks. We regularly visited the hospital for tests, treatments, and emergency visits. He was hospitalized just before Ana's birth. A friend who had assisted with the cleaning business quit. I alone carried the financial and work responsibilities. I was seven months pregnant. Nearly every day at work, I had to mop huge floors. It was very hard on my abdomen muscles. I continuously felt that I was dilating even more every day that I was actively doing professional cleaning for local businesses. I put in as many as 12 hours a day for a few days each week. One client was a gigantic church. I spent much time crying and praying to God there. I was not alone. There was an unborn, mystery child within me growing.

Somewhere in that vast cathedral, God was caring about us.

Ana Comes Into Our Lives

Two days before Ana was born, I could not get out of bed, so I was exhausted. When I went into labor, Ana arrived quickly, giving me a delightful and much-needed break. I loved every minute of holding and nursing her, and I was in awe of her beauty.

However, Ana briefly experienced newborn health issues. My parents took our older daughter Tia to their home for three weeks. On the third day after Ana's birth, we took her to visit one of my husband's work associates and his wife. Ana was sleeping in my lap, but suddenly she started squirming and turning bright pink - then purple!

"We have to do something! "I yelled, handing her to my husband and then heading to the old rotary phone to dial 9-1-1.

Ana passed out. The emergency dispatch directed, "Give her mouth-to-mouth breaths."

I translated, "Give her puffs of air!"

My husband was breathing into the baby's mouth, giving Ana air, and saying,

"Please, God, let her live!"

Moments later, the ambulance arrived. The paramedics took our baby and me by ambulance to the hospital. The paramedics gazed at her. I think they enjoyed this part of their job. By then, she was breathing on her own. She remained in the hospital's intensive care unit for newborns for a week of observation. I think she had choked on some phlegm.

We brought Ana home with a breathing monitor. Often, she struggled with phlegm and breathing, and I don't know if that had anything to do with her developing asthma later in her young life. When she was seven, Ana went to the hospital with severe respiratory problems. Fortunately, over time she gradually improved.

Tia, Our Sweet, Active Toddler

At almost fourteen months, Tia would bob her head and rock her upper torso back and forth to Rush Limbaugh's bumper music. She also did this when Ann Jel, an older cousin, set the tempo, saying, "Bah bah bah bah bum,…." She loved physically moving and would shake her entire body from side to side with her feet still. (She does that to this day.)

One day Tia found my pure corn starch powder. She put it up to her nose, and it smelled fresh! Then Tia paused and took a good look at it. Then she gave it another long sniff. Her curiosity kept her six senses busy.

She would go up to Sam (my mother's black half-Persian cat), touch him lightly, and walk a few steps away. A moment later, she would return and touch him lightly again as she repeated what sounded like "petty petty." Her fun with the kitty continued for minutes. Tia loved animals.

Years ago, I wrote down some characteristics of their personalities, and I cherish their differences.

> **Tia:** Before birth, she moved vigorously and actively
> **Ana:** Before birth, she moved rarely and easily
>
> **Tia:** Loud, hard, frequent crying
> **Ana:** Soft, gently building, infrequent crying

Tia: Needed to be held most of the time in the first and second years
Ana: Needed to be held the first six months; content to explore by herself

Tia: Very talkative
Ana: Very quiet

Tia: Ate well the first 1 and 1/2 years
Ana: Didn't care much about eating, spit food out; preferred playing

Tia: Upset and angry when things didn't go her way
Ana: Easy-come, easy-go much of the time if things didn't go her way

Tia: Interested in reading from three months of age – longer-than-average attention span
Ana: Interested in things mostly to look at and play with

Through thick and thin, my babies were my comfort.

I kept a notebook of Tia's movements before she was born. I enjoyed feeling the sensations of her stretching out straight when she was four months along. I kept track of the times and how the movements felt inside of me. I wrote down the times I felt her move. I learned later that the tapping she did inside my uterus was her hiccoughing. I worked security at a landfill gate. I had all kinds of time to sense what she was doing. It was a little bit ticklish having her growing inside of me! While Ana was coming along, I moved around a lot with the cleaning I did for our company. I cherished those days when they were secure inside of me.

Long-distance family life was often meaningful for us at that time. It was a special joy to see all the cousins twirling and dancing and bobbing in the living room to the delight of the grandparents! Holidays included extended visits and delicious feasts of our favorite foods. Often, we would eat moms' or aunties' homemade Norwegian Kringlas with butter. It was a nice escape from the usual daily stress. I loved seeing my relatives and catching up on the family news while taking a break from the everyday schedule. The girls loved bonding with extended family as well.

I would have gladly spent every day at home raising my daughters. That was my heart's desire. But I carried most of the necessary financial load because my spouse could not work much due to back problems, diabetes, and asthma. I became a financial wizard since he could not manage money. Despite my back pain following the birth of Tia, I took over the cleaning business duties while Daniel stayed at home for a while. He was having problems with a slipped disc in his back. Later, he got a job as a security guard. I got a part-time job as a security guard to supplement our small cleaning business's meager income. While guarding the gate, I got bored. I gathered snow to make a snowman inside the outhouse. The snowman's stick arm made the outhouse door open just slightly. It scared the supervisor out of his wits. Another day I built a snowman in the back of a worker's truck. Harmless pranks! I hid my mischievous smile. I read books, listened to the radio, and pumped milk for my Tia. I also spent time sewing and creating art in the guardhouse.

The Money Management Chaos

Daniel and I spent money differently. In 1993 (about five years into our marriage), I separated our finances into two bank accounts because the family budget was going haywire. I had one bank account that I managed. He had a bank account that he managed. I could no longer take the chaos of living paycheck to paycheck without measures to prevent overspending. I took care of the mortgage payments, insurance payments, and other essentials our family needed. Dan handled the phone payment, cable bill, and other expenses that (I felt) we could live without since he had trouble managing more critical accounts. I called him "the luxury man." We got separate refrigerators because he called our regular family groceries "survival" food. He put prime steaks and other expensive foods in his refrigerator. Dan rarely shared his steaks and other unique foods with the children. He would eat the food in front of them.

Dan had problems bouncing checks for several months until he finally figured it out.

The Tornados of the 1990s

It was the summer of 1992 when I was first pregnant with my youngest daughter., A major F5 tornado hit my parents' community. Their farm was about three miles from the renowned Chandler Tornado that wrecked the countryside and small towns. Other neighbors and relatives were affected by damaged property and injuries. It was the only F5 tornado that year in the United States.

In 1998 our town lay in the path of the F4 tornado that hit at the end of March, known as the Comfrey St. Peter Tornado. Our living room window was wide open. It grew very black outside, and I heard a roaring train sound - no trains came through our city anymore! The girls were already in the basement, and I was still in the living room, getting ready to run downstairs. The tornado touched down about three blocks from us, but we didn't lose anything. We were still struggling financially and didn't have homeowners' insurance. A few days later, we drove around reading written messages like, "Where's Dorothy?" and "Have you seen my underwear?" We laughed. People have a sense of humor even after such a tragedy.

Day-to-Day Problems

Daniel carelessly left dangerous knives on the coffee table in the girls' early years. I would yell angrily at his behavior. Another time, our furnace stopped running in November 1993. He turned on all the gas stove burners. It was good that we all didn't die from carbon monoxide poisoning. Thank you to Child Protective Services' help, who directed us to services to replace our furnace. Affording a furnace was impossible on our own!

I Was Hoping For Something Greater!

I knew my daughters were gorgeous. A hairdresser thought both girls could be models. I agreed! I sent photos to the New Faces Modeling Agency and got a response saying they wanted Tia to be in the book. She was so adorable with her tight Shirley Temple curls, charismatic, outgoing personality with beautiful round cheeks. We got a call to meet at one of the studios. Unfortunately, I got lost and was late, so we couldn't secure that opportunity. Another time I found an advertisement by Ford Models to come in for an audition. I had to get Tia ready for it. I was eager to see our family succeed with such an opportunity. I bought a rusty plaid pleated skirt, a matching top at Gap Children's Wear, and another outfit. I also got four airplane tickets to Chicago. Many hopeful people were there with their children at the Old Curtis Hotel. There was a runway showing children and their outfits for modeling agents from New York. Tia won the hearts of many agents with her bubbly, optimistic, friendly personality. She shouted as her name was announced as one of the winners,

"I won! I won!" Maybe we were scammed since we couldn't afford to move to New York. Tia was a winner in my world. It was an experience that felt real!

More of Daniel's Quirks

It was about a handful of years since Daniel had stopped wearing his wedding ring. The explanation he gave was unclear to me. He also put up obstacles to attending church, saying that "churches don't like us," although he did not explain why.

In one instance, Daniel mentioned that Tia needed surgery on her mouth. I was in shock over that statement. Her mouth is perfect with the most elegant curves, just like the ancestors on his side of the family. I defended her beauty. There is absolutely nothing wrong with her mouth. Indeed, there was something wrong with Dan!

When we all went to see the movie "The Passion of the Christ," there was an unusual display of moaning and groaning while waiting to get into the theatre. He held on tightly to Tia and Ana, and I watched in bewilderment about this bizarre behavior. All three were moaning and groaning!

Why Would My Dad Say Such an Awful Thing?

Once in a great while, my parents would take a 3-and-a-half-hour trip to visit us. I heard a rare, peculiar thing coming from my dad's mouth. I told my parents I worked nights at the box company. "What?" asked my dad, "You work nights? Your girls are going to grow up to be prostitutes!" I was so upset by this curse and the odd words coming out of his dark, dreary, devilish mouth. I was shocked into silence as usual. Why would any grandfather curse his young granddaughters like this? I thought way less of him than I had in my super low opinion before this.

I was outraged seeing the evil before my very squinting, unbelieving eyes.

Studying Art at the University of Minnesota

I had hoped to do something with art since that is what I enjoy! I was working the night shift at the corrugated box company. After work, I would drive to the Art Department downtown to create my sculptures. Dan didn't know where I was, so he called 9-1-1. He reported that I was a missing person. A couple of police officers found me safe and sound, working diligently on my art.

The following semester, I created ceramic sculptures with my fun teachers, Wheeler and Hoard. I made a giant, coiled Python that crumbled, a whimsical creature with sunken eyes, very long legs, and a set of five different types of shells. We were encouraged to build ceramic pieces that were higher than one and a half feet. Try it! It's a challenge! But don't be afraid if it crumbles. I got an A for effort and creativity!

I encouraged my daughters to play with the clay I brought home to work on, and I wanted to include them in my fun. I watched as Ana cried in frustration, "This doesn't make into a cup!" I had to calm and comfort her since clay cups shouldn't be a miserable experience. Art needs to stay FUN for everyone all the time!

Fun Times

We lived on a dead-end road. The girls would roll down the hill on skateboards, jump in leaves in the fall, and when the weather was nice, they would ride their bikes in the back alley.

Our TV was on from morning to night with cable channels to watch. The girls laughed at Sponge Bob and Earth Worm Jim.

I have always loved nature and found it a source of comfort and inspiration. One family joy we shared was when my husband and the girls came home one evening, where we saw a midnight rainbow in the sky created by the light of the full moon! They drove to the house to pick me up to find a place to view it. It looked as though instead of colors when you see one in the daylight. This one in the night sky had gray tints for each hue.

There was another thrill I enjoyed one night while hanging clothes outdoors on the clothesline in my underwear. At the north edge of our city, I saw the aurora borealis, waves of beautiful purple and blue lights in the night sky!

Often, I would take the girls out at night to watch falling stars or study stars in the dark sky where there was little city light pollution. One time the girls and I took a trip to my parent's farm in September 2001. I was used to being up all night, and I'd heard about the meteor shower coming. So, I got Tia up to witness it, and we enjoyed the wildest meteor event I ever saw! Seeing clearly and being in awe of God's unique creation was nice! I couldn't wake my younger daughter to see the extraordinary night-time display, and she was in deep slumber. Of course, my husband wasn't with us to share this remarkable historical display of numerous, fast, falling stars all over the sky; he avoided going on trips to the farm.

In the late 1990s, I bought a used 14-foot boat to take our family out on the local lakes for some fishing. My oldest daughter got hooked on fishing when she was six. One day I took both girls out on the boat for fun. Tia was thrilled, but Ana cried.

We would go to Seven Mile Creek Park to enjoy the beautiful scenery and walk through the creek or the trees on the hills. Parks often filled our time because they didn't cost much but a bit of gas to get there.

In January 1995, I began working at the Corrugated Cardboard Company, which would continue for the next twenty years. The work was very physical. Doors were wide open in the summertime, with high humid temperatures in the eighties and the nineties. Mosquitoes bit all of us employees while we were working hard. Sometimes animals, moths, butterflies, birds, bats, salamanders, spiders, and frogs would make their way indoors. This farm-raised girl was not afraid of these critters. It amused me that they were around. I grabbed a box and scooped up a genuine, live Minnesota gopher to surprise some guys working in a nearby area. They yelled and got out of the way while the lady on my three to four-person work team was screaming! After work, I whisked the gopher away and released the box-chewing critter in a nearby park.

Distractions like these sure relieved the boredom in our hectic workplace. One night, a privilege we experienced was when we saw a beautiful Luna Moth flutter about our workspaces. A few of us tried to catch it - with no such luck. Another time, a Pink Spotted Hawk Moth made its way inside, and my Asian co-workers pleaded for me to be careful not to hurt it. I shared their respect for all those creatures. Another time several of us studied a bat hanging around a high-piled stack of cut corrugated cardboard. I was always happy to be relieved of the constant boredom whenever a fascinating creature came through. I loved to talk, but the work area was too loud, and hurried to converse much or take it easy, as we had to work hard and quickly. But the money and company benefits made our little family of four secure.

I worked lots of overtime. For a while, I worked twelve-hour shifts daily for several weeks at a time, with Sundays, holidays, or vacation days off. Occasionally, I would take a rest break and work six eight-hour weekly shifts. I was delighted about getting ahead with the bills. I believed my husband, and I were a team taking care of our precious girls. The home loan interest rate with the local bank was over 8.0 percent. I paid off the little one-and-a-half-story house with my bank accounts at age 45. My financial plans were finally coming together.

The girls were my biggest blessings in life. I enjoyed watching them learn and grow. I often bragged about them in my letters to my mother, who fully understood. My daughters were my shining stars. I wanted to be with them all the time like my mom was with us growing up.

I have cherished a couple of cute memories of Ana:

1. The day she went outside in the gravel driveway with only her diaper on. She wasn't much more than one and a half years old. I followed her out. She joyfully jumped up and down in a mud puddle where our van wheel had dug in. What an opportunist when it comes to something fun! I smiled and still do over that scene where the next-door elderly neighbors saw it too!

2. Another favorite memory is when Tia and Ana were interested in birds. I took a picture of them holding a stick with a baby blue jay, ready to learn how to fly. We had a mama blue jay sitting in her nest right outside the upstairs window for years. The girls were around ages 8 and 10. Tia was always very observant. I had gotten her three different bird guides. She was serious about studying them. She also had extraordinary eyesight to be able to learn them!

One summer, Tia had a Have-a-Heart animal trap to catch the many critters that came to check it out. Many cats went into the trap, and once there was a skunk. I looked out the window to see the black and white striped creature! I had to get rid of the skunk, but I hate to kill anything, so I threw a sheet over the trap and loaded it into our old white car with a rusted hole in the trunk. I drove several miles into the country to let it loose. That skunk smell stayed with me for a long time!

Tia kept occupied with many creatures, including two smelly ferrets. Our house was filled with a rat, hamsters, gerbils, a pet corn snake, a couple of dogs (a mastiff/ St. Bernard giant male dog and a very defensive, unfriendly German Shepherd mix), and some cats. Tia kept busy, and home was where her heart was most of the time. Tia had to put down the mixed German Shepherd. He was only three years old, and he was awful for children. There was no choice. Tia lost the only grandma she ever had, her young dog, and a favorite special black cat named Midnight, all in September 2011.

Special Notes From the Girls That Always Make Me Smile

From Tia, when she started writing:

> MOM! I cudent see you bkuss I'm tirde
> MOM! Wake Me up! We will go fishing

From Ana:

> Hey mom, I went to spend the night at JoAnna's house.
> – Ana

Like many parents, I have a stack of pictures they created and words they wrote. I smile and fondly remember those sweet moments when they were so young.

Winter days here in Minnesota are crazy cold. One January morning, I looked out our bathroom window to check the thermometer, which was 30 below zero! That didn't even include the wind chill!

My husband wrote a note one December day in 1999.

> Aren,
>
> It's going to be 30 below with the wind chill. The van is all gassed up with super unleaded. That will help stop gas line freeze up. Don't forget your winter survival kit. Do you want to call when you get there? We'll probably be asleep, but I'll answer the phone. And more important, call before you come home. It's going to be cold, subzero, for two days, then warm up to the '20s on Wednesday and '30s by Friday.
>
> Dan

————————

I felt he cared about my safety and appreciated it very much. I felt loved.

Around 2001 I took a black-and-white photography class. The following summer, I took a 35 mm family picture of us and a frog we caught by Circle Lake. The movie camera was also running. The frog jumped up in the air while we were posing, and I caught it in my hand. Every time the girls decide to watch our home movies, they get a big hearty laugh from the picture scene where we included a giant Leopard frog for a day!

CHAPTER 6
Family Letters

During my marriage and childbearing years, staying in touch with my family was an important comfort and guidance source. Looking back over these letters to loved ones so many years ago, I cherish those days when I could share day-to-day life happening in my world.

Mom also enjoyed being around children. She worked at a child daycare until she was 70. She was awarded a certificate from the State of Minnesota as a working senior. The children loved her, and she loved her job. When Ana was born, Tia went to stay with my parents, and mom took her to the daycare center where she worked. For three weeks, Tia stayed with them on the farm.

The following are random snail mail letters I had sent to my mom, dad, sister, and her family on the farm:

December 12, 1990
Hi Mom, Toady, and Ann Jel,

The baby could be here any day. Sometime within the next three weeks, I'd say. The doctor noted that my cervix is dilated to two centimeters. When it gets to four centimeters, that's when active labor might begin. Dan confided to the doctor that he might be quite nervous.

I love that he's able to express his feelings. I'm quite nervous, too, not knowing for sure how this is all going to go. So far, I'm hanging on to my regular work schedule. I'm going to work up until labor if I can make it.

I should get around to making cloth diapers with Velcro. Dan's dad is helping us with a car seat. They can be so high-priced. I need a baby lounge chair – remember what Ann Jel used to sit in – I'm not sure what it's called. Toady, can I use it?

Dan and I are going to learn some breathing techniques this and next week – whether or not we actually use them is the question.

———————

December 13, 1990

Do you like the name Jeremy or Matthew? What names do you like, especially for a boy?

Dan's dad went to Panama this week. His mom and dad are in their nineties. The last time he was there to see them was in 1986. He'll be gone for two months. The weather is probably in the eighties. Dan said his dad had gone to Panama once before and returned speaking Spanish to Dan and his brother. When Dan was down there, he said it was like being in a different world – his uncle said Dan was welcome to stay with them when Dan could speak Spanish fluently. What an uncle! Right?

There are interesting birds in Panama. One of them sounds just like a robin – it is green instead of orange like ours here. There are other interesting birds and animals – a red-headed lizard. These are the only ones I've heard Dan talk about.

I know it's Toady's birthday. I haven't been to the store to buy her anything, like a card. All I can do today is think about how old she is and how awful a sister I am for not letting her know that I know she's pushing 30.

Love, Aren, Dan, and?

December 25, 1990

Hi! Mom, Toady, Glenn, Ann Jel, Dad, and Matt, It's Christmas!

I'm still working on getting used to our new bundle of responsibilities. It seems so far, the only time she cries is when she's hungry, has bubbles in her digestive system, or her bonnet is falling into her face. She's very hungry. She lost a lot of weight and is down to about seven pounds. We had to bring her back to the hospital. She had a serious case of jaundice that she had developed since we brought her home. They put her under lights to get the waste out of her and pushed a lot of fluids into her. Dan and I stayed overnight with her in the hospital. This took place Thursday, December 20.

I'm back to work today. It's very easygoing. When it's this cold, we don't even make any key rounds – just watch the gate. I wrote Tia's story today. I made her some lunch for tomorrow. I think Pat used a milk machine. It sure helps to know something about cows. Now Tia's dad can take care of her and get a solid relationship going, as I've wished for.

Dividing our responsibilities should do us all some good. I wouldn't mind not working and would just like to be a housewife. But Dan offered to get a third job. I think it would be insane. Tia and I would never see him. I just felt it wouldn't be fair.

Little Tia makes horse snort sounds and rolls her tongue.

She also makes circular motions with her left arm and chases the right side of her head with her eyes. When I look at the right side of her face, she looks like you, Mom! She has Dad's nose. I can't wait to have you meet her. So, when are you coming over?

To help her get rid of jaundice, I've chased the sun's rays around the kitchen, dining room, and living room. She's been getting her little footies poked with needles and blood drawn for more than a week. Poor baby. Her bilirubin level has been up and down. I hope her misery is over soon. Dan said he couldn't bear to watch her get poked again.

When Tia was under the hospital lights for jaundice treatment, she tried to pull off the goggles that protected her eyes. The nurses were amazed that a newborn had such good hand coordination and strength. She improved greatly after about five days of lights and lots of water to drink.

Tomorrow, the 26th, we've been married for three years.

I called Rhonda last Sunday to tell her the good news. She was busy Christmas wrapping with Ashley.

Love, Tia, Dan, and Aren

P.S.

We got another little place to clean. We're getting good use out of our yellow page advertising.

I feel like my abdomen is splitting. There are purple stretch marks, I noticed. My ankles are swollen.

My car just had a birthday in Shakopee by a water tower today! Our Chevrolet Chevette turned over another 100,000 miles, and we are celebrating!

I just read on the bulletin board by one of the nearby buildings here at the dump that a Holstein cow owned by Bill and Melvin Brockberg from Edgerton, MN, has a MICKEY MOUSE MARKING that, of course, she was born with. Guess where she's going? To DISNEYLAND to the children's petting zoo.

I love the Christmas music they've been playing on KTIS. I still listen to Dr. James Dobson and Chuck Swindoll. Dobson talked about teaching children to be kind. We, adults, need to help the child that other children pick on for whatever reason – their looks, mostly. We need to defend the underdog and scold other children for treating this one badly.

Chuck Swindoll talked about the need to be sure of your source. Beware of those who say, "God told me."

Beware of those who look for signs: "If the next four lights are green, I'll go into the mission field."

"If she wears red plaid to the party, then I know that God wants me to marry her."

Beware also of those who say, "I got this from God in a dream."

So don't look for signs, don't look to the stars, don't look to dreams and visions. Today we're to understand and apply the truth, which of course, you know, is the Scriptures where we can gather God's will. I had been puzzled about the will of God in my late teen years, remember?

"Whatever is pure…" I'll have to look it up. Also, fruits of the Spirit: LOVE, JOY, PEACE, PATIENCE, KINDNESS, MEEKNESS, and SELF-CONTROL. I forgot a couple. If our lives include the Fruit of the Holy Spirit's actions, of course, we're in God's will. Loving God and loving others is another form of God's will. Of course, you have this all down pat. Yet, I find it fun to discuss.

July 1999
Hi Mom, Hi Dad!

Thanks for your letter. Thank you very much for the birthday card!

I've been praying for you. Any improvements?

Yes! I'm making plans to go to the Barnes family reunion. It's always fun to see Henry and all the aunts, uncles, and cousins.

Maybe, but not sure yet, we may bring a friend or two of the girls along with us. I haven't asked for Monday the 26th off, but hopefully, they will allow me to take it. Since I work days instead of nights, I'll be able to go back Sunday evening if they won't let me have Monday off.

Well, we got some rain. I have finally got some of my garden in. I still have to get tomato and pepper plants yet, and maybe even some more, oh yes, cucumber plants.

I'll see you soon!

Love,
Aren

———————

July 6, 1999
Hi Mom,

This thank-you note is very late – I apologize. Thanks for the books and such for the girls. It kept them entertained. Thanks for my flute.

Yes, we can work something out so you can go to church with us. We'll be going on a Saturday evening.

My sleeping schedule has changed since Dan has been working as a patrol officer. I sleep from about eight to four, but I can arrange to get up a little earlier if you come over in the early afternoon. I could also show you some of the sculptures I've made. I've had a lot of fun forming things with clay.

Can you think of anybody who would love to have one or

two Siamese cats? Dan loves his cats and thought of you to consult. One day I was going to take them up to the feed mill in New Market, where a lot of homeless kitties go, but he couldn't bear to part with them. So, he said to ask you. The one Siamese cat has been de-clawed, but I think he'd be a pretty good pet if he were neutered. He's about two to three years old, but we're not sure how old the mama cat is. She did have kittens this year, but they did not survive past a few weeks.

You know that Tia has a black cat that she loves very much, and Dan does not seem to have an allergic reaction to him.

See you later!
Love, Aren

Jan 26, 2005
Hi Mom!

Thanks for calling that one Sunday. I was selling at two local electronics stores.

Ana says, "Hi!"

Tia says, "Hi!"

Tia has been helping a blind, autistic boy with bowling. She hands him the ball and helps him aim.

They are going to have the final Special Olympics games in February.

I have been shopping for plants to put in my yard for extra beauty. I'm looking forward to gardening again too.

I read a lot almost every day. I enjoy web surfing.

Dan is considering a job change. He wants to work part-time and get on disability.

I'm having problems with the water pressure tank. We are looking for somebody to fix it. It's depressing. It will cheer me up to be able to have water go directly into the tub.

Hope to hear from you soon.

Hope to tell you good news about the water tank.

Love from Aren

February 20, 2005
Hi Mom!

We sure have a snowstorm going on! It's very nice to have a day of rest today.

Yesterday I was giving out granola bar samples. Marjie stopped in the store to buy a few groceries. She asked how you were.

[continued letter two days later - February 22, 2005]

Ana's been sick with a sore throat. She has a fever, too.

Well, it's probably going to be decided today. A tug of war for over the years. A husband wants his wife to die. The parents want her to live. The only things she needs to live are food and water.

I've been shopping for plants. I hope to do some landscaping. I'm probably going to get Angel Trumpets, Hibiscus, and Fuchsias. I hope to add some beautiful flowers to my yard.

How's everybody?

Any good news?

I'm still making plans to go to Aunt Ginny's birthday party. I hope the weather is good.

Love,
Tia, Ana, Dan, Aren

———————

May 2005
Hi Mom!

How do you like this print? They call it Verdana.

Well, I'm still spinning in circles like you used to do. If I could go at airplane speed, I still couldn't keep up with everything I had to do. So, I gave up and decided to tell you how crazy my life is.

I know that it would be a lot less hectic if I didn't want or need anything. I did buy the water pump at Fleet Farm. So that's done. Now Dan and I just need to take the time to sit down and put it together.

Ana is talking about going to school next fall. I'll have to get enrollment forms. I hope it goes well for her. I hope her "in-school" experiences are far, far better than Dan's or mine was. I always want the best for my girls. Tia can get her high school diploma by following the school credits form I have in their school file. She's highly creative, and going to a "school" might squash her creativity. She does a lot of reading. She comprehends things. I didn't comprehend as much as she did. You should see all the things she reads.

Ana still loves to draw, draw, and draw and uses her computer for a good part of the day.

This weekend I have a Yoplait yogurt demo to do on Saturday and a vitamin demo on Sunday.

Tia just told me that Trixie, our dog ripped open her paw pad. I just got back from cleaning her wound, covering it with antiseptic, and wrapping it up.

Now I'm off to the post office with your letter. Yes, I got your letter. Thanks!

We'll keep you posted on what's happening here. Oh, Dan got a newer van. It's a plum color. It's really pretty!

Love ya,
Aren, Dan, Tia, and Ana

(added to the same envelope. I typed huge bold letters for mom so she could see the words.)

Hi Mom!

This is Elephant Script! Do you like it?

I have still been busy with my landscaping plans.

Lately, Tia has been studying the 17 species of snakes in Minnesota. 2 of those are poisonous. She sure has a fascination with creatures of all kinds. Ana draws, draws & draws just about all the time!

Well, I've been up late reading & having too much fun on this computer again.

Love Ya, Hope to come visit you soon!

Love Aren, Dan, Tia & Ana!

———————

The letters fill me with sentimental nostalgia for the good times and love shared among our extended family, even at a distance. I am so grateful for these mementos that remind me of how supportive and generous my parents and siblings were. When things went wrong in my marriage, they were our broken families' continual pillars of strength.

CHAPTER 7
Discovering Child Sexual Abuse in the Family

Family incest is often tricky to detect. Abusers are sly and discreet and threaten with consequences or bribes with gifts. It's confusing to young children, who usually do not know how to talk about what is happening to them. They believe that incest happens in every family until they learn from their friends or other relatives that this is not how families should behave.

The other parent wants to believe and trust that everything is going smoothly within the family. There is no reason to ask or accuse that parent of wrongdoing without specific warning signs or evidence to reveal the other parent's criminal acts. Sexual child abuse can sometimes continue undetected for years. When a child comes to you about sexual abuse, it is essential NOT to shame them or blame them for what they describe.

Their father told my daughters not to talk to anyone about the abuse. Their father warned them that authorities would remove them from their home, school, family, and friends. Threats of punishment and repercussions silenced my children. Their father told them to keep secrets. Shame and fear kept them from telling anyone. No one ever saw their father do anything inappropriate to either of them in public or around other family members and close friends.

However, the children's enforced silence was as abusive as the physical assaults. Not allowing children to talk about what's going on never helps them. They should be taught about good parental touching and wrong or inappropriate touch by a family member or adult. They should learn this by a gesture or simple vocabulary before they can talk. As early as possible, children should know the basic terms for the human body and normal functions versus abnormal activities to inform a responsible adult of inappropriate behavior by another adult.

If a concern should arise, someone in the family who is watching the children might prevent a perpetrator from potentially harming them. The responsible parent can organize a team of family members to keep an eye on the children to ensure they are safe from inappropriate contact with an adult. The team should watch for signs and symptoms of child abuse and inform the responsible parent of any suspicious behavior. Boundaries must clearly indicate what is acceptable versus unacceptable parent-child physical interaction and dialogue.

Abusers are sneaky and deceptive. Everyone around the children must be on their toes, watching like hawks for anything suspicious. Training young children to understand the nature of inappropriate behavior toward them will empower them to recognize a problem and report it before it goes any further.

Unfortunately, despite my goals and good intentions, I thought wrong when I believed that my husband and I could do the job of looking out for our children and their safety. I assumed he and I followed the same family values and moral behavior code.

In my family's case, hospital workers were the first to identify the problem and notify law enforcement. The ambulance took my thirteen-year-old Ana to the hospital's emergency department for treatment following a medication overdose. Her closest friends immediately saw the problem and learned that she had taken several pills that turned out to be aspirin. The friends called Emergency Responders, and they transported her to the hospital.

Two or so months before Ana attempted suicide, she would sit silently in the easy chair with an angry look on her face. I tried to talk with her, but she was overwhelmingly absorbed by something churning within her tormented mind. It puzzled me to no end. She refused to speak.

I was shocked to learn of my daughter's medical condition and mental state and the source of her issues, the many years of her young life during which her father had sexually abused her without my knowledge.

I saw how much she was crying at the hospital, and I was crying too. I knew I had to tell her that none of the chaos with her dad was her fault. I called her on the phone at Mayo Teen Suicide Center. I believe it helped her a little to know how I empathized with her confusion and pain. I told her I loved her. I drove to see her every other day or called her on the phone. She was at the hospital for almost one week.

Our priority was to consult with doctors to ensure my daughter would be okay. Fortunately, they were able to treat her physical condition and get her stabilized. The next phase was more difficult. We would need to work with several mental health professionals to get my daughter the help she needed to begin a challenging recovery from her traumatic experiences. It would be a long road, but her sister and I were committed to supporting her during the complicated process. Her father – who was also her abuser – appeared to be upset and worried, but I questioned whether his motives were mixed and somewhat selfish. Did he fear his incestual pedophilia would be revealed, forcing him into legal proceedings and a probable prison sentence? No doubt that concern was behind some of the vivid emotions he displayed at the hospital and after that.

After hearing about my daughter's abuse from the hospital staff, I came forward to law enforcement to say what I had learned. Immediately the consequence of correction started to roll furiously fast. There were interviews, testimonies, and investigations. Investigators and medical professionals finally uncovered a great deal of information to reveal the horrendous abuse my two daughters had suffered over many years. I was horrified to hear what had happened to my precious girls in our home through their father's illicit and immoral sexual abuse. Although I was distraught by my daughter's suicide attempt, I was also grateful that something good came about from this. Through her contact with experienced professional doctors, nurses, and social workers, she released years of shameful secrets that had been torturing her and her sister for most of their lives.

After the SWAT team hauled my husband away to jail, I went into our house with the officers and found some strange things like a long note Dan wrote taped to the computer:

Aren,

I can't begin to tell you how sorry I am for bringing such pain upon this family. I wish I could do something to make everything alright. I wish I could back up time. Please tell Tia and especially Ana I'm sorry, and I love them dearly. I love them more than life itself. (And that ain't no lie) If I could kill myself and make poor Ana feel better, I would. I need to see the Doctor to get documented evidence that I have disabilities. What medications I'm on, and for what. I may not get my asthma meds or insulin if I have to live somewhere else.

I guess most of all I'm sorry I lost your trust in me. My life is over. This is not a suicide note. But if I have to leave this family, I only have one place to go. And with the only job I can do gone, I'll have to live in the streets. And with my medical conditions, I won't last a week.

I just hope you guys and the Lord forgives me. Because how do I forgive myself? You probably don't want to see me again, and that is understandable, but I need just a little help from you. I'm going to have the Mayo clinic send up my medical records on me. I'm also getting medical records from Park Nicollet. I need you to keep these in a file for me.

I wish there was some way I can do to make amends. I just hope Ana can recover from this. I do love you all very much.

Aren, please don't change the phone number. I need to know how Ana is doing, how you all are doing.

Aren, please don't divorce me, although I deserve it. You're the only one who ever loved me, and you're the only one who understood me. You're the only woman I could ever love. And despite my shortcomings, I have always loved and cared for you and the girls. Making their birthdays special for them. Worrying about them. Keeping them safe. Tia's leather coat. And I left Ana my cell phone with a note happy birthday on it. You will have to buy a card for it before March 1st. I tried to be a good husband

and a good father, otherwise.

May I write you?

Dan

I felt so many tangled up, twisted, and extra overwhelming emotions with that note. So many questions like "Was it so difficult for Dan to avoid this colossal-sized mess?" "Was it compared to being tempted with an irresistible cookie in a cookie jar?" I was crying and confused. The whole event threw me into the craziest emotional loop ever!

Another strange thing is that I found a hunting gun covered in my bed upstairs. Dan was alone for a few days while the cops waited for him to come out of the house. The dogs relieved themselves in the basement. The hamsters died during the time we were gone. That was the chaos I saw the day Tia and I returned home. I learned later from his friend Phil that he was considering suicide, and he talked Dan out of it.

I had grabbed a few factory-made boxes from work, perfect for all the medical paperwork, news clippings, and social work papers. I called it the 'Living Nightmare Box". I wished it didn't exist but could do nothing about it. It was filling up fast and full of papers.

During the long and stressful recovery phase, I learned a tremendous amount of child sexual abuse information by reading endless articles on the world wide web. Although shocked about some things, I began to understand its causes and effects, and I learned how to support my young daughters as they worked through the healing process they so desperately needed. Anyone who becomes knowledgeable on an important topic can become an authority. Community presentations, seminars, and work-shops for local groups of parents and students and educating people who work closely with children can be among the most effective solutions to preventing the typical silence and secrecy surrounding child sexual abuse.

Child Protective Services directed medical, psychological, and individual evaluation support. I started having conversations with social workers. In one case, the victim's mom denied help for the victim. The abusive father was a well-known business-man, and the mom would have felt the crush of numerous finan-cial responsibilities without him. There was difficulty convicting him since the mother didn't come forward with the apparent truth. She may have been aware of community resources, includ-ing financial support, that would have been available if she had left her husband. I believe that she was in denial even though the truth was right before her eyes. She probably told herself that the elephant in the room everybody was seeing did not exist. Noth-ing to see here!

When I talked with one of my elder daughter's friends' moth-ers, she informed me about how one teen attempted suicide. The mother shamed her and went as far as not believing her. The girl was sexually abused by her father.

In another situation, a young male teacher who was a volley-ball coach at my younger daughter's public school sent home car-nations with all the girls. He used a closet for sexual encounters with one young teen girl that other girls referred to as a "slut." She was a victim under eighteen; I emphasized this to my daugh-ters and friends while driving to volleyball practice one day.

Later, I got acquainted with a lady at the Loaves and Fishes

Community meals, where she told me that the prison counselors tested her IQ at 157! She spent about six months in prison. Her boyfriend, not the daughter's father, was incarcerated for several years. Her mom's boyfriend and mother sexually abused her young teen daughter. This mother has been on parole for over 20 years. She lives with guilt over how things developed and how she wanted to please her lover. I feel that she is sincere in doing her best to care for the young grandson who lives with her. Her daughter has been permanently affected, living a chaotic life with the numerous men she meets and gets intimately involved with them.

Although this issue is difficult to discuss and deal with, it needs to get out in the open. Staying quiet about sexual abuse and incest does not cure the problem. I have found helpful information and will continue to search for more answers to this terrible problem. From what I have learned, I believe my ex-husband got involved with some evil influences. He had a friend who slept with his mother, another friend who slept with his sister, and still another older friend who slept with his daughter and faced no criminal charges. I learned these details while getting my ex's things back to him. He just told me, "I thought I could do this. " when talking about abusing our daughters.

It was shocking to hear this confession. Daniel believed he could commit sexual crimes like his friends and probably wouldn't be caught or punished, just like those who got away with their criminal behavior. Some of those friends dabbled in drugs, and Daniel nearly died from using hog medicine (PCP) and Heroin.

They lived dangerous, reckless lives, and unfortunately, their wrong thinking and illegal activities caused harm to innocent victims, including my two beautiful daughters.

I texted (spring of 2020) my former husband, who served his prison time and now lives in a different city, asking directly: "What is a clear answer to why people get involved with pedophilia? "

He answers very few of my questions, and other times he doesn't answer at all. Recently (2021), I boldly asked, "Is there a type of punishment that would have stopped you from being inappropriately close to the girls? For instance, the death penalty, if it did exist? I'm curious!" Surprisingly, he answered, "I like how you put that inappropriately close. I was, my brother told my mother. Do you know what she did? She called me names like queer and that I was sick. But do you think she got me any help? No. But if I knew how prison would be, it may have de-toured me."

"Thank you for talking to me about how you felt," I responded. "Discussing various topics is a great interest of mine. I enjoy being a problem solver," I added.

Twice just a few months before Daniel got out of prison, I asked for an order for protection at two different women's crisis centers. Twice I was denied. The counselors at the women's centers said a judge would not consider the request. There must be two or more reasons to be granted an Order For Protection. I wouldn't be talking with him now if I had the OFP. The court ordered me to return his coin collection, music albums, and clothes. I eventually had conversations with him to determine what to do with his belongings. It was awkward to contact him, but I faced the enemy head-on. Yet, I'm still mystified about his secretive and sinful behavior. I thought I knew him, and I had loved him, and his betrayal broke my heart.

Daniel revealed some things about his counseling sessions with other pedophiles in a recent message exchange. There is a woman in his group. After a few more months of counseling, Dan will be "graduating." He told me that the counselor would allow me to join the group to learn about the behavior and "treatment," and for the group members to learn something from my perspective as a victim.

I volunteered to be a "watchdog" for Dan. I made up this title because I did not get specific permission to talk about the "treatment" in detail. I recently learned that I would be meeting with a counselor and Dan to be a "watchdog" to help make sure that, for instance, when attending the 4th of July Fireworks, it is precisely that and nothing involving minors. " Th-That, that, that is you. I am completely honest with you." I replied, "Okay, you can be honest with me." Then he added, "The next thing it says is your "watchdog" needs to attend meetings with you and the counselor.

Attending a group meeting would still be interesting, and I have not been invited to one of those yet. Perhaps I can ask a counselor when I see one. An excellent reason comes to my mind why pedophiles need a secret, safe, anonymous place to get the help they need so everyone will benefit!

I learned that Dan's little brother was the first victim of his inappropriate touching. I was disturbed, surprised, and haunted by this reveal. It happened when they were ages 5 and 10. It went on for a few years. In another instance, he pulled down a girl's pants and fondled her. She was 14, and he was 18. He referred to the early times in his life when he and other children played "doctor." When the discussion of our children came up, he explained that he was angry with me for something and "took it out on the children." He also denied the report that came with a polygraph. He said it wasn't accurate. After explaining his anger toward me, he charged me with the question, "Why didn't you have an orgasm when I was inside you?" He changed the subject abruptly. He was defensive, I would say. That was a surprise question I wasn't expecting. His reasons for abuse made sense to him, but I have concluded that it is senseless to people who are wired right. I thought it was more complicated than that.

He explained that he had a powerful sex drive, which I already knew. But if you need stimulation, there are sex toys to use instead of children and other people! Can that be a solution?

He explained that he had been faithful to me but then decided that he had cheated on me with the children. He concluded that he was responsible for taking care of them for life. Then he said he wanted to give them a large inheritance. I'm thinking, "Okay, that sounds nice." Of course, I wish he would have made an excellent choice, like respecting the children!

One day before we got on the elevator, I noticed his legs shaking, and he said, "Don't you hate me?" I said, "I wasn't built like that." I was facing the enemy and the truth because I was still trying to get how this stupid, inappropriate behavior worked! I will learn more as life happens. I do hate INAPPROPRIATE TOUCHING and the damage it does to people!

I admitted to officials that I lead a hectic life and would not always be able to check on him, and I suggested that there could be other family members to be his "watchdog." The therapist said that Dan would ultimately be responsible for his behaviors.

I commented that Dan should focus on the 55-plus age group, being he is in that group. We talked about the senior center and other clubs that seniors belong to, and I stated that he needs to ignore all youth when it comes to anyone other than seniors. Years ago, while dating, I often heard him comment on the dress, hairstyle, attitude, or how a teenage girl said something. Then he would say, "She needs to be slapped!"

Dan and I went to chat more, sitting on separate benches a few feet from each other. I was asking about how difficult something like incest is to avoid. "How can it be avoided?" I questioned. Daniel believes that certain people are born with an incestual nature. I should have asked, "Born with a sinful nature? Isn't that what the Bible says?"

He talked about a friend in prison who was in the "same boat." Two daughters were victims, and he also had faith in God. Daniel said, "and he only got five years, and I got 15" (Daniel was in prison for ten years for good behavior).

I believe that a perpetrator of a sex crime doesn't ever get enough institutional time! He talked about the sex offenders in prison who stole the children, raped them, and killed them. "Everybody hates those!" he commented.

He talked about cellmates that would tell him all about making crystal meth or how to crack open a safe. "I don't want to know anything about making meth! I don't want to know anything about cracking open a safe!"

CHAPTER 8
Tia's Story

I was a complete tomboy. My big, blonde, Shirley Temple-like hair was always a wild mess. I wore boys' clothes most of the time because they were comfortable and cool-looking.

My mom grew up on a farm, and we spent a lot of time there as kids over the summer with Grandma and Grandpa. Their home and fields were a safe haven because my grandparents and my dad never got along, and he didn't care for the long drive, so he often stayed home. I remember waking up early and running out the door as soon as I could get my shoes on.

"Don't you want some breakfast?" Grandma would always stop me in the cheerful kitchen before I ran outside.

"No, thanks!" I was always too excited to eat first thing. Outside, I would play with my grandparents' huge St. Bernard dog, and he'd follow me around everywhere I explored: run-down barns, cow pastures, the chicken coop, and rabbit hutches. I explored every inch of that farm and enjoyed every day spent there. It was our favorite getaway.

At home, I'd spend most of my time in our backyard, either in the vegetable garden or climbing mulberry and pear trees that grew beside the shed.

Who My Father Was

In a few words, he was hateful, perverted, unkind, short-tempered, and above all: vile.

Dad was an extreme conservative. I remember him watching CSPAN, screaming at the TV that someone should shoot a Democrat senator or two in the head after he became angered by their policies. He often said he wished he could walk into a Planned Parenthood and "take care" of all the doctors with his Second Amendment right. Dad was also a conspiracy theorist. He was misogynistic and violent; his anger always lay in wait for me to trigger it somehow through a wrong tone of voice or occasional messes that my sister and I made. He needed a target to vent his poisonous hatred, and unfortunately, his two young daughters were the most accessible and vulnerable.

When he became enraged, my sister and I would often get slapped in the face or whipped by his hand or by vacuum cords, wooden feather duster handles, or anything hard within reach. The vacuum cord was by far the most painful; I could hardly breathe through the lashings.

My dad owned a cleaning company. My sister and I would go with him to clean office buildings late at night, usually working from 9 p.m. to 5 a.m. at various business and shop locations. While at work, Dad would often have us stand up on boxes in closets so he could molest us.

What He Told My Sister and Me

When helping him clean offices, he frequently referred to me as "half-a**ed Tia" because my cleaning skills weren't great at such a young age, so he would scream that nickname at the top of his lungs, as no one else was around. Verbal abuse or physical abuse came as punishment for not completing work tasks to his liking. I recall one time hearing his muffled screaming through a mask he wore to sort the dust from the grain in the factories. But he never gave us small girls protective masks to wear.

Sexual abuse was the worst. Before taking me into his bedroom to molest me, he'd ask, "It's okay, right?" as if asking permission, all the while repeating, "Remember that I asked if this was okay" to set up an excuse if he should ever get caught.

Just before he would climax, he would tell me he loved me over and over. This was one reason why hearing that statement from people who actually cared about me didn't sit well and was something I had to work on because when he whispered that slime into my ear, I knew it wasn't true. This led to my having a hard time believing anyone could honestly say that to me.

"No man will love you if you cut your hair short," my father warned.

"No man can touch you but me until I give you away to your husband," he insisted.

"You'll get fat if you keep eating; you're a bottomless pit," was his frequent criticism, even though he was obese.

Once I went to pick something off the floor, and he commented my 'gut' was "hanging low like some fat a**."

Every day felt like I was walking on eggshells, hoping he wouldn't lash out and call me names. I'd hide and eat in a different room so he wouldn't make fun of my weight because his taunts happened often and got worse as I matured. He used to tell me I needed to be skinny like my sister, or no man would find me attractive.

"No man would..." he would often say, which translates to "men like me."

Five Years Old

When I was age five, we started going on cleaning runs with Dad. Often, we were up all night. My sister and I hated it so much because we'd come home from a long night of cleaning with him, and we'd want nothing more than to play outside in the sunshine or see our friends. The more I think about the way we lived, the more I realize we lived that way so my dad could keep us away from other people as much as possible because of his fear of getting caught. He would often tell me no one but him was to be trusted, not even my mom, and he would drill into our heads all the horrible things CPS would do to him if he were caught.

He asked, "You don't want them to take you and your sister away from your mother and me, do you? They'll separate you and your sister." Fear worked well on us because we were children.

Ruled by Hate

I have a memory from when I was around six years old of my dad watching a show on TV with me, and he would pause it at any shot of a young girl or boy and stare at it, then start kissing noises at the still image. These were moments I knew he was about to pull my sister or me, or both of us, into his bedroom. Certain programs would trigger a sexual reaction from him, and us being within arm's reach was too easy. Whenever my dad wanted to communicate that he was about to molest us, he'd ask if we wanted a 'whole lotta candy,' as he would buy us a candy bar after each time it happened. He used this phrase in case we ever said it out loud so Mom wouldn't know what it meant. Dad sometimes had one of us stand guard for Mom outside the room while he molested the other.

My dad lusted after young boys. What's interesting is he supposedly hated gay men or anyone who belonged to the LGBT community. I believe this was because he had hidden gay tendencies but was a 'devout Christian' and therefore pushed those feelings down with the only emotion that ruled him: hate. He even had a light blue t-shirt made that he wore proudly with "I hate faggots" printed in bold black letters on the front.

When I was six years old, my mom started taking me fishing after I expressed a real interest in it. I remember taking a large stick I found in the backyard, tying a string to it, and attaching a hook that I had found in my dad's old tackle box. I caught several bullheads with that silly makeshift pole.

Circle Lake was where my mom, my sister, and I spent much time walking around the water's edge and catching frogs. My sister and I lovingly referred to it as 'the frog-catching lake.' Those were fun times that represented the better parts of childhood.

The Cats

When I was seven, what I remember most was the way Dad treated cats. Dad had caught a female Siamese cat that was pregnant with kittens. He went on about how beautiful this cat was and how he wanted to breed and sell beautiful cats just like her. As soon as she had her litter of kittens, we found half were Siamese-looking, and half were all black. He told my sister and me he only kept beautiful things like those Siamese cats and us, and the 'ugly' black ones didn't deserve to live.

Every day, when I woke up, I would run downstairs to where the kittens and their mother were kept to play with them. One day I rushed downstairs to find only the Siamese kittens with their mother and the black ones nowhere to be found. I ran upstairs to ask Dad, and he told me that they were downstairs in a bucket. I ran back down to the basement to find a bucket with a lid on tight and opened it up to see them. I picked up a small, limp, and lifeless form. Turning around to my dad standing behind me, I asked what had happened to them.

"Black cats don't sell, and I need to make money. I put them in there last night so they could suffocate to death."

I had never cried so hard in my life. My dad picked a male Siamese kitten from her litter to breed to its mother since, in his mind, they would produce more Siamese cats to sell. This didn't go well, and most kittens died because of inbreeding. I remember my sister had picked one incestuous kitten that she really loved, but the kitten ended up dying because they were all weak and sick. She carried the dead kitten around for a day before our dad made her bury it beside the shed in the backyard. Many failed litters of kittens were buried there. He continued breeding Siamese cats, and one litter after the other, I'd watch him kill the black kittens by drowning, suffocation, or sometimes dumping them in the river or dropping them off in the country. There was even one litter of black kittens that he killed by force-feeding them antifreeze. Every time I begged and cried for him to spare their lives, but I was never successful. The female cat eventually got old, and he finally stopped trying to breed her after many, many failed attempts.

This was not the only incident involving cats. He would catch feral cats in a live trap throughout my childhood and drown them in a tub in the basement while my sister and I watched. I remember feeling numb seeing those cats stick their paws through the holes in the trap, watching their bubbles rise. I wished so much that I could help them, but I was terrified of my dad. I was helpless.

Drowning wasn't the only way he'd hurt feral cats; he once left one in a cage to starve before shooting it with a bb gun. I vividly remember a trail of bright red blood running down the cat's perfect white fur.

Dad repented quite often. He'd wake up screaming from a nightmare about how if he was hurting Ana and me, God should "smite" him, but nothing ever happened, and he'd just go back to abusing us. He often used religion to justify his actions (hating gay people and molesting his daughters. He also brought up the biblical story of Lot and his daughters).

The home I was brought up in was a nightmare in itself. I distinctly remember dirty dishes that sat in stagnant water in the sink filled with rotting food for weeks. Maggots, flies, and moths were everywhere in the home, and it was only cleaned when neighbors called CPS. Stale air and piles of junk-filled the rooms; it felt like suffocation. I felt no stability growing up. As a child, I felt as though I were floating through time, waiting. I was just waiting to go somewhere else. Somewhere clean, warm, and safe.

A few months after Dad was taken into custody, I sat on the couch and watched a few home videos of my sister and me as children. Dad was the one who recorded most of those videos, and after hearing his voice in the background of the home movie, I decided to pause it. The house was calm and quiet, the sun was shining through the curtains, and my black cat, Midnight, was laying on my lap purring loudly; I felt an overwhelming peace come over me as I muttered, "I'm free", under my breath. And it was true, at that moment, my life was beginning. All those moments as a child when I knew I was waiting for something, waiting for something to give, waiting for that peace I knew would come to me. I waited for years, and my peace finally came.

My life has changed drastically compared to my childhood, and I have my friends, my mom, my sister, and my own resilience to thank. These days I find true happiness in raising my son, taking him fishing, being outdoors, listening to my Pink Floyd albums, practicing my painting, and even playing video games. I've been employed at my full-time job for going on ten years, and I have built some pretty incredible friendships with people who only want to see me succeed. I wouldn't change a thing about that.

Today's world seems just as chaotic as it was years ago, but with a different kind of chaos. Now we see movements like #MeToo emerge, and as a survivor of sexual assault, I feel it is incredibly important to lift up survivors and give them a platform to use their voices. It is important to believe survivors, especially if it is a dear friend or family member. I've heard rebuttals to that statement, and I understand where the disagreement may come from, but let me be clear: it is up to the court and our justice system to determine the truth of any given case that is brought before them, and it is up to you as that person's friend or family member to support them whether you believe them or not. I am lucky that my mom believed me, and it is disheartening to hear how many survivors are not believed.

In the words of comedian Patton Oswalt's late wife, Michelle McNamara – "Everything is chaos; be kind."

For the duration of my young life, I tried to rely on my

parents for support, and I tried to rely on religion for support. Sometimes those who you expect will step up and save you are the ones who will fail you, as human beings tend to do on occasion, parents or otherwise. Sometimes you have to save yourself. You need to have a desperation to live life fully; you need to realize you deserve more than what you're going through and more than who's putting you through it. Take no shit from those who seek to destroy you, and say 'no' loudly and unapologetically. Be wildly and naturally you, and life is sure to follow.

Escape

My dad often made remarks about who or what did or didn't deserve life. One time at a restaurant, seated at the table just across from us was a disabled boy with Down syndrome. My father said, "Those people should all be put down like animals; they are a drain on our tax dollars."

His hateful remarks disgusted me. Even as a child, I knew these terrible statements directed at certain people were wrong, and I remember feeling horrible hearing the things that came out of his mouth.

I had grown up with very few friends, having been kept out of school for obvious reasons. I could only hope to keep friends from church or around our small town. My three best friends at the time were siblings. Being friends of the family, my mom was good friends with their parents, John and Carol. Their children, Jerry, Junior, and Carrie, were my best friends. Carrie, being my closest friend, there were so many times I wanted to tell her, so many times I just wanted to cry on her shoulder and reveal all the horrible things I was going through. I daydreamed about telling her parents and begging them to keep my sister and me. They were a normal, happy family in my eyes, and I wanted nothing more than to be part of it. Luckily, I was allowed to spend lots more time with them as I got older. Some of my fondest memories are with that family. I was always safe with them, and I have much to thank them for.

In my childhood eyes, this family was wonderful. Most importantly, they were kind and offered a helping hand whenever my family experienced some sort of tragedy or hardship. Once my dad was having heart trouble, and an ambulance was called. It must have been almost four a.m., and my mother needed to go with him to the hospital. I remember being awakened and rushed outside where Carol was standing, ambulance lights flashing in her face red and blue, and her warm arms welcomed my sister and me, her soft voice calming us as my dad was loaded up and taken to the hospital. She took us to her home that late night and let us share her children's beds. That family does now and will continue to mean the world to me.

John took me fishing with the boys. He would make sure to help me bait my hook correctly and take the fish off the hook, which he still does to this day, and he included me in everything from learning to clean a fish to explaining how backing and launching the boat from the dock was done. John gave welcoming hugs and words of encouragement whenever he could. He was the kind father figure I so desperately needed.

Carol was lovely. She was a strong and incredible homemaker and a fiercely protective mother. If you knew her, even though she had only birthed three, she had dozens of lost children that called her Mom. Sometimes I would sit in the kitchen with her and talk for what seemed like hours. Even though I am no longer a religious woman, she always and to this day reminds me of the woman in Proverbs 31:

[10] "A wife of noble character who can find? She is worth far more than rubies. [11] Her husband has full confidence in her And lacks nothing of value.

[20] She opens her arms to the poor And extends her hands to the needy.

[25] She is clothed with strength and dignity; She can laugh at the days to come. [26] She speaks with wisdom, And faithful instruction is on her tongue. [27] She watches over the affairs of her household And does not eat the bread of idleness. [28] Her children arise and call her blessed; Her husband also, and he praises her: [29] 'Many women do noble things, but you surpass them all.'"

Jerry was quite a bit older than the rest of us kids and very involved with sports and his friends. But when he was at home, he'd often humor his younger siblings and us by playing Jedi and Sith Lord with us, hide and seek, and showing us how to play card games like Magic the Gathering because he was a bit of a nerd. He loved and cared about his brother and sister as any older sibling should.

Junior was the middle child. He loved laughing at anything and everything he found funny and enjoyed making my sister and me laugh by any means. He was the pioneer and leader in all our imaginative play and would often come up with a game or scenario we could play out on the spot. He loved swords and lightsabers and collected dozens of figurines and dinosaur toys, openly sharing everything with us so we could play, too.

Carrie was the daughter. She loved her kitty, adored playing dress-up and doing nails, and shared both with us as well. When ever we girls put on dresses and painted our nails, we would drag Junior out of whatever he was doing and make him play dress-up with us. We made him the prince while we got to be the princesses. He was not usually amused but went along anyway.

Our small hometown had a yearly summer festival with parades, food vendors, and plenty of games and farm animals. It was basically a county fair. In the summer of 2003, I desperately wanted to go as I had a crush on a boy I knew would be there. I wasn't allowed to go for one reason or another, and I begged my dad for days leading up to it. The evening before the festival, I was awakened from a nap by my dad crawling into my bed. He whispered disgusting things in my ear, and I recognized his tone of voice. He told me if I wanted to go, I knew what to do. I was able to go to the festival in exchange for being molested for what was the last time, as I got my period a few weeks later. I didn't think about it at the time, but I realize now that having my first period was my saving grace. Before that, he often made me exchange social events with my friends for sexual favors.

As I got older, I started getting bolder in my interactions with our dad. Frustration, yelling, and fighting all went hand-in-hand with most conversations. I had developed a deep hatred for him, and it showed. I fantasized about his death and how free I would be if his poor health finally took him. He had been hospitalized and had two or three severe heart palpitations by this time and was very obese, with diabetes and asthma.

I wanted so badly to leave the house as often as possible, but I had to ask Dad every time. I wasn't allowed to get permission from my mom, only Dad.

When I was 15, one of my friends asked me to go up north with him and his family for camping and four-wheeling. When I asked my father, he laughed and said, "No, he's a man and a ginger one.

I don't want ugly grandchildren. Besides, you don't get to stay the night with boys; that's just not what people do."

I replied, "F**king your daughters is another thing people don't do."

He let me go on that camping trip with my friend and his family. My dad often made inappropriate statements like the one about my guy friend being a redhead and me "f**king" him and having "ginger babies." He frequently commented on my friends' physical appearances.

My sister and I loved going on evening walks together around our tiny town. We'd walk and talk for hours; it felt like heaven because we were free outside the house on our own, a much-needed escape. Walking, talking, and fantasizing about what life would be like without Dad became our main conversation. Soon, it was all we talked about on our walks: escape. How we could do it, what would happen if we did, and how we planned to stick together. We were becoming more and more desperate. Winter came, and our walks stopped.

Life Changes Forever

By age 16, I had become very involved with the church. I had gone to youth group with our family friends one night, and right after service, I got a call on my friend's cell phone from my dad.

"My baby tried to kill herself, "he screamed into the phone. His voice was shaky, and I could tell he was sobbing. "Have John bring you to the hospital in Northfield. They have her there."

The drive to Northfield from Prior Lake felt surreal as if it took days. My best friend, the only person who truly understood me and my pain, was in pain herself, so much that she felt she couldn't take it anymore, and the only way out was death. My mind was numb, trying to figure out what had happened to my sister and how I could help.

I finally got to the hospital. My mom and dad were waiting to go in as I arrived, and the doctor called on us to go back and see Ana.

She looked exhausted, her hair was a mess, and her eyes were sunken. She was staring at the floor when we walked into her room. The doctor explained that Ana had taken a large number of painkillers in an attempt to end her life. We were told we could visit for a while, but she'd need to be kept overnight and likely admitted to a hospital specializing in suicidal teens.

Mom and Dad talked with her for a while, and when they were done, I asked if I could visit with my sister alone. The doctor ushered my parents out, and as soon as the door closed, we made eye contact.

"Tell them," I said.

She looked at me and nodded. We knew it was time.

All those talks we'd had on our walks the past summer boiled down to this moment. I knew that if she told her therapist and the doctors while hospitalized that I needed to be the one to tell Mom. I walked out and left with Mom and Dad after saying our goodbyes.

A day or two later, the three of us drove down to the hospital where my sister was staying in Rochester. I had my new iPod with earbuds and stared out the window, thinking, wondering when my moment would come to tell Mom. Had my sister told someone, or could she even bring herself to say anything?

In the hospital, I was instructed to stay in the waiting room while my parents went to speak with the doctors and psychiatrists.

I waited and waited until, finally, they came out. My mom spoke a bit more with the doctor. My dad looked far away, and my mom seemed concerned and on the verge of tears. We walked out to the car, and during the drive, I had my iPod headphones on but no music, so I could hear them talking. Mom and Dad discussed how the doctor had told them that my sister had been diagnosed with PTSD due to alleged sexual abuse. The doctors didn't tell them anything more or who had allegedly done it, so my mother was trying to drag out of my dad what he thought.

"It has to be that new boyfriend of hers, right? Who else could it be?" She kept asking.

My dad remained silent until he yelled, "In America, you're always guilty until proven innocent!" He sounded not the least bit concerned that Ana was in the hospital for trying to hurt herself and was more concerned with being "falsely accused," which no one had done yet, but he knew the truth, and so did I.

I held my tongue.

CHAPTER 9
Shock and Regret

If I had been able to tell ahead of time that my future husband would be a pedophile, I would have steered clear of him. I knew about pedophiles, but I had no clue that one was part of our family until Ana attempted to end her life with several pain pills. This tragedy should not happen to anyone.

Because these behaviors are seldom openly discussed in society or families, it can be challenging to discover sexual child abuse. Becoming aware of my children's mistreatment was one of the most traumatic events I've ever experienced. It mentally tore me to pieces by imagining everything my dear daughters went through. I became outraged and embarrassed beyond measure. Seeking professional help, a family doctor tried to connect me with another woman who had experienced the same criminal acts on her children. I made an effort to contact her, but she never responded. The social workers were also unable to organize a group for talk therapy, which might have been beneficial. Fortunately, I was able to receive individual treatment. My daughters participated in both group therapy and individual therapy. We also undertook family therapy for a few weeks.

We started with a faith-based counselor. After two sessions, the state-certified psychologist determined that my older daughter was stable. My Ana participated in counseling for several weeks, as our social worker felt this was an essential part of her recovery and healing process. At that point, the faith-based state-certified counselor determined that Ana had finished counseling.

When I reported this to our social worker, she firmly fumed, "No, no, that is not enough!"

I figured the counselors knew what they were doing. I didn't fight with my social worker and decided to go to the clinic where I got my annual physical. There was also a counseling department at the same clinic. A second opinion would prove itself, and it did. I connected with my social worker's favorite, Mr. P. (one of our second opinion counselors), a state-licensed psychologist. He became angry and verbally abusive and insisted that my older daughter was hiding something. He was very angry with the faith-based counselors and gave me the third degree!

I was upset! All the counselors were state-certified, but the second set didn't think the original counselors knew what they were doing. I decided to get both girls into sessions with the counselors in the health care system that I used. We went for a few weeks, and the girls took the MMPI psychological test to determine their state of mind. The second-opinion counselors only administered the MMPI, but the diagnoses proved to be the same as the faith-based, even without using the MMPI test.

This test showed that my older daughter was stable, while the younger was defiant and depressed. The faith-based counselors were first to determine the diagnosis. Nystrom counselors also had an M.D. on staff who diagnosed my youngest daughter's PTSD and Major Depressive Disorder conditions.

I went along with what the social worker wanted, but I thought she needed to let the counselors with the certifications make the diagnosis and recommendations.

After two months, Ana wanted to quit counseling. I told Ana that it was necessary to discuss this with the Ph.D. counselor who had recommended counseling for two years.

The highly recommended, angry, fault-finding Counselor Mr. P., whom the social worker raved about, verbally beat me up about the faith-based counseling center and claimed I was influencing my daughters to abuse children in the future. He said that he was going to report me to the authorities. I felt mistreated and victimized. I did have a problem being on time anywhere, including counseling appointments. This counselor became hostile, and I quietly left that session like a dog with its tail between its legs. My younger daughter expressed that she wanted to quit counseling sessions. I told her that she needed to discuss this with the counselor who had recommended counseling for two years. However, she successfully ended the sessions after two months.

A few months after the revelation of abuse, my older daughter Tia made a drawing of the three of us in the few counseling sessions she had with Mr. P. She drew Ana, herself, and me like wolves. She put me at the top of the page. Then she penciled herself and Ana as wolves beneath me in much greater detail than I. This artwork was an essential part of my older daughter's therapy. It was intriguing to see how she drew our new family of three in a natural state. Tia is a canine lover! I had taken our family to the International Wolf Center in Ely, Minnesota, a few months before Daniel's unexpected incarceration, for an educational experience and because my daughter loves anything canine. I had no idea that our visit to that park would influence her to depict us like wolves in the wild following our counseling sessions!

During this time, I had another sort of problem! The family dogs escaped! Just that moment, I needed to get ready for work. I took the dogs out to go potty. Suddenly they seized the moment of freedom and took off running! I could not get them to come back. I felt the urgency to get going to work. I was not the kind to not show up at my place of employment. It was a dilemma, for sure! The neighbors were understandably furious when the dogs dug through their trash. I should have stayed home that day! I got a misdemeanor charge of "dogs at large" and a fine of $185.

I felt deserted. The husband I had married was not the loving, caring man I thought he was. He had tricked me. He had defrauded two beautiful gems, our girls. I had to find a way to carry on despite this severe damage. Often, I so very much wished it was a horrible dream I could escape. But the disaster could not be righted. My children had helplessly suffered under his control for years.

As the reality of sexual abuse came into the spotlight in 2007, I struggled on several levels. Everything was unbearable. I felt as though an earthquake had struck our family. Being without a partner was hard to get used to since I had to take on even more responsibilities. It was lonely. Everything was painful because of the weight of my children's suffering, the ongoing financial issues, and the sense of betrayal by my spouse, who I had trusted with our children's well-being.

When the crime of incest materialized, I felt crushed and over-whelmed. While therapy helped somewhat, the girls and I needed more income and a new place to live. The girls begged to move away. I wanted to, but I could not afford it because we were technically in poverty. The girls and I improved the house's interior by ripping out the carpet and painting the walls a colorful "Summer Pudding" that was popular. We also cleaned out unnecessary things, but there was still too much stuff in the house. I had hoarded too much from garage sales over the years.

Going to work was difficult because many coworkers knew what had happened, and I hung my head in shame. People gave me piteous looks everywhere I went, and I felt down, embarrassed, and cried nearly all the time. I wanted to be happy, light-hearted, and carefree from problems, and I wished the horrible dream would be over soon.

It would have been wonderful to share the love of a man who would have taken care of the girls and me, and I would have bragged about how he was successful and a great dad to his children. I saw many families where their relationships appeared to be healthy. Maybe I was envious, but I admired them for the successful family life they enjoyed.

Was I mad at God? Not one bit. I had been angry with God for something simple in my childhood, like the chickenpox scar between my eyes. Now, I was sure that Jesus was in tears over this tragedy and for any disaster on earth. Jesus wants things to go well for us. But then there is the free will factor.

I needed a man that left the toilet seat up, the toothpaste lid off, or forgot to bring flowers for a special day. I could be happy with a man that couldn't manage money as long as I could be in charge of that. I could have taken a man that didn't attend church services regularly or one that was so very busy with his career that he didn't have time for me. What many women dislike in their men would have been paradise. But instead, I got a man that deceived me and used our precious children, not for love, but for perverted and evil control.

CHAPTER 10
Court Trial

My husband faced criminal charges for both daughters' abuse nine months after being taken by a SWAT team. A court trial took place regarding several counts of abuse against Tia and Ana. Below is a transcript of the proceedings.

STATE OF MINNESOTA

****

DISTRICT COURT

THIRD JUDICIAL DISTRICT

****

State of Minnesota, Plaintiff

Vs.

Daniel Ross, Defendant

****

[Legal Attorney for the State of Minnesota on behalf of our family is named as well as Legal Attorney / Public Defender for the girls' father-abuser, who is present in Court]

[Transcriptionist is Named]

****

THE COURT: Back on August 7, 2007, you plead guilty to counts 7 and 8, which were added as part of the plea agreement, and you pled guilty to two separate counts of criminal sexual conduct in the second degree. Count 7 related to your daughter with the initials T. R. and count eight your daughter with the initials A. R. The Court ordered a pre-sentence investigation, victim impact information, which I've received and reviewed. I note from the sentencing worksheet it shows you have a criminal history of zero, and this is a severity level seven offense, and the guidelines provide for a 90-month commitment to prison with a 5-year conditional release. And I believe that the issue of whether its concurrent or consecutive sentence are permissive under the guidelines.

[Defense Attorney], you received the information, reviewed it with Mr. Ross?

DEFENSE ATTORNEY: Your Honor, we did receive the sentencing worksheet as well as the PSI that did contain a psychological assessment performed by the expert. Ah, we have reviewed those documents together.

However, when I came back in the courtroom after meeting with my client downstairs, I was presented with three victim affidavits or statements – which we have not yet reviewed together. We're in the process of reading those right now. Your Honor, we are prepared to go forward.

THE COURT: All right. And just for the record, Mr. Ross, you have read those victim impact statements?

THE DEFENDANT: Yes.

THE COURT: All right. And the Court has as well.

[Assistant Defense Attorney requests Assistant County Attorney substitute for him for the remainder of the argument, which the Court allows]

ASSISTANT DEFENSE: The, um, Minnesota Sentencing Guidelines have changed the way we sentence in Minnesota, where the Courts don't have as much discretion in a lot of areas.

But one area where the Court has complete discretion is in the area of whether or not to sentence consecutively or concurrently, where the Sentencing guidelines call for permissive consecutive sentencing.

There are permissive — there are presumptive concurrent, and there are presumptive consecutive. This is neither one of those.

This is a permissive consecutive where it's completely up to the Court whether or not these two charges should be sentenced concurrently or consecutively.

And Plaintiff's Attorney, on page 6 of the pre-sentence investigation report, makes, ah, some rather interesting arguments as to why it should be consecutive: Ah, the position of authority as the victims' biological father; his, ah — his imposing physical size relative to these small children; the fact that the acts constituted numerous acts over an extended period of time and far more than is required for the elements of the crime to be met; ah, the victims' tender years during this time from the age of 4 all the way up to 14; the continuing psychological impact on the victims; the, ah, presence of the other victim while one victim was being molested.

All these factors, ah — I mean, to read these factors, it almost sounds like an argument for some kind of aggravated departure.

And that's not what we're asking for in this case. We're not asking that the Court go beyond what the guidelines would normally call for. We're simply asking that within the range of what the guidelines considers to be reasonable that the court adopt the more severe sentence, the more severe sanction of sentencing these two counts consecutively to each other.

The law and the guidelines provide for 90-month prison terms for each of those two sentences. The question is simply whether it's going to be consecutive or concurrent.

The balance, in this case, starts off flat; if you will, there's nothing on the either side under the Minnesota Sentencing Guidelines to suggest that it should be consecutive or concurrent.

But in this case, the State argues that the balance does tip toward consecutive for six different reasons. Number one, we had two separate victims. Ah, this is a case where there is no sanction, no real sanction for that second victim if the second victim's offense is sentenced concurrently.

Second, as Plaintiff's Attorney said, this was an offense committed countless times from the age of – from the age of 3 or 4 through puberty. These children were in their tenderest of years, and the victim took – or the defendant took advantage of his special relationship to them to victimize them during that time. There were two childhoods ruined – two childhoods ruined by this defendant. And it's appropriate that two 90-month sentences should be imposed.

Um, fourth, although it appears that the abuse was primarily characterized by contact as – as the crime indicates, it also sometimes appears to have gone beyond to penetration, and also it seems it was sometimes done in the presence of the other victim, as Plaintiff's Attorney points out.

Five is that unique betrayal of trust with respect to both victims.

And sixth is looking at the practical problem of whether or not the defendant can complete sex offender treatment within a 90-month period of time.

Now it is certainly possible, and possibly even probable, that the defendant can complete sex offender treatment within a 90-month period of time. Ah, the – if you look at the psycho-sexual evaluation, the defendant is described as taking minimal ownership for his current offense and described certainly as needing some kind of in-patient sexual offender treatment program.

As the Court is aware, there is a process for preparation for that program. It takes considerable period of time to get into that program. Um, the program itself will take a considerable period of time and then monitoring afterwards. All of that will take a considerable period of time if everything goes well.

But we have the defendant taking minimal ownership for – for what he's done here. Um, Plaintiff's Attorney informs me that if something goes wrong with the defendant's treatment program, it is possible for the whole process to get re-started and have to go back to the beginning of the treatment program, which will take more years.

And as the Court knows, the defendant has been in custody since he was arrested in January, so he has significant credit for this offense. He, ah, you know, assuming he gets good time, he's only looking at a few years here to finish all this sex offender treatment. Ah, he could do it if everything goes perfectly.

But if everything does not go perfectly, um, there's a significant risk of the defendant being released at the conclusion of his prison term untreated. That is, I think, a serious risk that the Court should take every measure to avoid. And can avoid, I think, virtually eliminate the possibility of the defendant being released untreated simply by doing what I think is otherwise eminently justified under the facts of this case, which is to say two consecutive 90-month terms.

Thank you, Your Honor – Your Honor, I guess at this time, if the Court has any – and I don't think the Court normally does, but if the Court has any questions of me, I would ask that the Court give them at this time since I'm about to leave.

THE COURT: I have no questions. But I'm going to allow the victims to make their statements at this time.

DEFENSE ATTORNEY: Thank you, Your Honor.

THE COURT: You're excused.

DEFENSE ATTORNEY: Thank you, Your Honor. I will be followed by Mrs. Aren Ross.

THE COURT: All right. Ms. Ross, will you come up and be seated at the counsel table next to the Replacement Defense Attorney so you're close to the microphone. All right. You may give your statement.

MRS. AREN ROSS: Okay. I needed a father for the girls that would treat them respectfully and not as objects for his convenience. I needed a father for the girls that would nurture and protect them, not turn them into victims of child prostitution. I'm not certain to what extent (crying) the crime affected the girls' well-being. I'm sure they were confused about normal fathers and normal relationships. This crime has affected me to the point where (crying) I find myself in tears (inaudible). The girls were inappropriately touched, physically injured. Yes, the girls were each emotionally injured in different ways, and they wanted to kill the pain by killing themselves. Tia has been angered by his behavior. I have been emotionally, psychologically horrified, and shocked this January about the crime he committed, knowing all the damage he has done (crying) – to Tia and Ana, and it has put me into a depression so great I'm not certain that I can recover. My world has been turned upside down. The girls have been severely affected by a decade or more of his damaging behavior. They were physically and emotionally battered by the way he treated them. The crime has put our lives out of balance. I wish this was some way to gain restitution for the girls' sake. The victims are paying the price again for his failure to be gainfully employed and financially supporting his children. (Inaudible) more he won't ever harm a child again. The girls would be better off to never hear from him or see him again. I'm not sure when or if I should hear from him by writing; I'm not sure the conversation would be pleasant. I don't know what to do or what would be best. I continually cry over the whole traumatic scene. I thought he and I thought alike. I was betrayed and deceived.

THE COURT: All right. Next.

REPLACEMENT DEFENSE COUNSEL: Your Honor, Tia, and Ana would like to make their victim impact statement as well.

THE COURT: All right. Please come forward one at a time. Start out stating your name, please.

TIA ROSS: I am Tia Ross.

THE COURT: All right. And why don't you pull the microphone right up in front of your face there? You're difficult to hear.

MS. TIA ROSS: This better?

THE COURT: Thank you. Go ahead.

MS. TIA ROSS: All right. Sorry, but this is going to be kind of long.

All right. Um, hello, Daniel. It's nice to speak with you

again, or should I just skip all that and say just kidding?

I'm a little disappointed to tell you that I'm extremely relieved that you're gone. Would you like to know why? All right, let's go. How about we start with the fact that I now get to actually spend time with my friends? And, yes, JoAnna is my best friend. And I will be telling you that for the last time.

Let's second that with one of the things that is probably the worst. You never showed Ana and I what a true Christian father would do. You would also point people out and judge them according to your own little scale. And by the way, a sin is a sin, so if you care to know what a real Christian is, I suggest you take your Bible, start in Genesis, and work your way to the back.

You know what else I hated? Seeing Ana's attitude dramatically change when you walked in the room. It ate me up inside seeing how much hate you made her feel and how much hate you made me feel towards you.

Another thing I couldn't stand was knowing that you knew what you had done and didn't care one ounce how it would affect mom.

By the way, she's a better parent than you ever were. She lets me go out into the world and set my own goals. Speaking of which, guess where I went. To Connecticut. I bet you'd like to know why right? Well, I went to see a boy. Yes, that's right. I have a boyfriend now, and I love him very much even though he's so far away.

Anyways, I got there by bus and met up with him and his

parents at the Greyhound bus station. And I went through downtown Chicago, Pittsburgh, and, yeah, the Big Apple, that's right, I went through

New York City alone. Remember how you said I had to be a man to travel alone? Well, guess what? I'm still a woman.

Oh, and guess what else, you're never going to see our children, your grandchildren, ever. Like what you hear? It gets better. You're not even going to get a chance to see a photo of them, those cute little blue-eyed, blond-haired children.

Oh, anyway, I forgot to tell you, um, he's nothing like you. He's pure of heart, respectful, Christian, the whole nine yards. You know what? It makes me happy to describe the person that you'll never meet. You don't deserve to meet him. Although I'm pretty sure he will beat you if you come near our family. And, yes, he knows what you have done. He's furious, just as everyone else is. And I know he would protect me if you ever tried to find us. God help you if you do.

By the way, my man and my friends support me more than you ever did.

And Ana and I are closer than ever. It's too bad you'll never hear us laugh and joke again. And it's too bad you'll never see mom again. She's much better off without you.

But what did you expect? So many things in our lives have changed for better because you're gone. We no longer have to come to you and ask for everything before we did it. We no longer have to hide in our rooms because you'd gotten home from work. We no longer have to hate weekends because you were home all day.

And best of all, we're free. Anyway, I'm going to leave it at that and say goodbye. It's too bad you don't know me anymore.

THE COURT: Ready? Please state your name first.

MS. ANA ROSS: Ana Ross. Do I start now? Hello, Dad – right, I mean Daniel, because I don't really think you deserve dad as your title.

I'm a lot more stable than I was on January 10th; I believe it was. But I grew up a lot since you've gone away, and a lot of things have changed in my life like I have a new boyfriend, and the town has changed, and the house has changed because we're actually doing what we want without being in such a choke-hold that we can't breathe.

You know what else? It's not my fault, Tia's fault, or mom's fault that you're no longer here to know any of these things. It's yours.

And I'm not going to tell you my new boyfriend's name or anything about him, or even why I broke up with Tyler. I'm not going to tell you about how Lenni looks different. I'm not going to even tell you how the house looks because you should have been here to know yourself.

And, you know, when or if I get married, you're not going to be there to walk me down the aisle like you said you would.

You know I still draw. I'm getting really good at it. It actually looks realistic now. Too bad you'll never see them.

You know, some days I despise you, some days I miss you, a lot of days I just forget you.

What's sad is that it makes me happy, sad, angry, and disgusted that you're gone. I'm disgusted because what you've done to this family is detestable, especially in God's eyes. And you got your sick pleasure from a two-year-old.

I get sad because of how you've taken advantage of your authority as a parent. It makes me sick.

And now I'll never know what a real father is because you never knew what that meant.

I'm angry because you have hurt mom so much. And to see her in pain and cry most nights breaks my heart.

You know you have knowingly done this to her. And I'm happy because now mom no longer has to deal with you, you and your statements of "I'm the man of this house, I make the rules. " You know, I despise when you make that excuse that you can do whatever you want because you're a man. And when you think about it, it's kind of funny because every time I told you not to lust at other women because you were married, you'd always tell me I have a right to be a man.

Look where that statement got you. Do you think you've taken that statement too far yet?

You know, I have more friends since you have left because

all of your screwed-up rules that make no sense aren't there anymore.

And now I don't have to hate 2 o'clock any more, you know, the time you got home from work. Yeah. My mood actually changed every time you pulled in the driveway because I knew I'd have to listen to you because you were still an authority figure of this house.

That's another part I hate. You had authority. I hated that because I felt – wait, I feel you never deserved authority. And all you did was sit on your throne as the man and fill your face full of food that you were too selfish to share.

Hey, there's another thing I hate, you're selfish. That to me is why you're even in this mess because you know you're — your selfish desire — sorry I lost my place -that to me is why you're even in this mess because you know your selfish desire of that addiction has led you to this.

And also now, thanks to you, guess who my very first memory is?

Yeah, you showing your love for your addiction. You cluttered up my supposed to be happy childhood memories.

Well, I just wanted you to know that, Daniel. I hope you're happy with the decision you made over the past ten years because now you will never see, hear, or talk to me, mom, or Tia.

THE COURT: Counsel for Plaintiff, anything further for the State?

PLAINTIFF ATTORNEY: No, Your Honor.

THE COURT: Counsel for Defendant?

DEFENSE ATTORNEY: Thank you, Your Honor. Your Honor, Mr. Ross does appear before the Court with regards to sentencing with regards to two charges of criminal sexual conduct in the second degree.

Underneath Minnesota Sentencing Guidelines, it calls for a commitment to prison for a period of 90 months. With good time that would require him to serve at least 60 months' worth of time.

As my colleague has pointed out, the question really becomes whether or not the Court under this circumstances is going to look at sentencing Mr. Ross to either a concurrent sentence or a consecutive sentence. Your Honor, we believe that the more appropriate course in this action would be a concurrent sentence. The reason for that, Your Honor, is you will take a look at the psychologic assessment that was completed in these matters. Although his characterization is that Mr. Ross takes minimal ownership of this offense, Mr. Ross will tell you to the contrary that he takes full responsibility for his actions that led to his convictions of these two matters. At no time has he ever placed any blame on the victims in this matter or anybody else. He's always placed it squarely upon himself. He's never minimized his involvement in this matter and has taken full responsibility for that. Now my colleague has indicated to the Court that one of the reasons you should look at consecutive sentencing is because of the fact that Mr. Ross might not be able to get the necessary treatment in prison should he be released at an earlier date. I think Plaintiff's Attorney fails to appreciate, um, the mechanisms that are currently available for sex offender treatment in the prison system.

First of all, Your Honor, there is a facility that he will probably be immediately transferred to that deals strictly with sex offender prisoners that's going to be up at Moose Lake.

Second of all, with his amenability to treatment, as indicated by the report, that Mr. Ross isn't going to probably face the initial denial that many of the offenders face when they go for treatment. It appears that he's acknowledged the extent of his behavior throughout his life so that they aren't going to be hung up with him, having denied any of the victims in this particular matter.

Um, we believe that with a 60-month actual time served in prison, there is plenty of time in which to be able to successfully complete the treatment programs that are currently available.

With that said, Your Honor, should he not have completed his treatment by that time, there would also be a 30 month parole time over his head, which I have seen many times that the conditions of parole are that they either continue with their sex offender treatment or alternatively, um, remain in an aftercare program to be monitored for their success outside of the community.

You will note, Your Honor, that the psychologist's testimony does indicate that Mr. Ross does represent a low risk of future re-offense. That's done not only by his own personal assessment but as well as the current risk assessment tools that he utilizes in making that decision.

And likewise, we do want to point out that it appears that Mr. Ross is amenable to treatment and believe that that's to his benefit.

As Counsel has pointed out, Mr. Ross was in custody since the time that this matter came to light back in January. As a result, Your Honor, we believe that Mr. Ross is entitled to 262 days of actual credit for jail time. I believe that carries us up through today's date. And unless the Court has information to the contrary.

THE COURT: Well, the Court – the Sheriff's certificate indicates 253 days which runs from January 17th, 2007 to today.

DEFENSE ATTORNEY: Okay.

THE COURT: It should not include today.

[Defense Attorney requests the Court to give Mr. Ross prison time credit for time served, to which the Court agrees following calculation of time served to date]

DEFENSE ATTORNEY: Your Honor, as you can imagine, having been incarcerated since that period of time, um, has put everything that Mr. Ross has in jeopardy as far as financial conditions are concerned. I was appointed as public defender in this particular matter because he is looking at a lengthy prison sentence in this matter. I would ask the Court, under the circumstances, to look at impos-ing a statutory minimum fine in this matter as well as as-sessing a $28 co-pay relative to that matter.

Lastly, Your Honor, we are urging the Court to look at concurrent sentencing in this matter. Um, Mr. Ross has a number of health problems that are spelled out at page four of the PSI in this matter. He's got diabetes. He's had asthma. He's got a heart condition. He's got lower back disk problems. He had bleeding stomach ulcer, colon cancer in `98 and suffers from arthritis. He takes a number of medications.

To be honest, if you sentence him consecutive in this matter, he's probably looking at a death sentence.

Because of that, Your Honor, even the concurrent sentencing is likely to take a heavy toll on him, and he'll be fortunate to be able to complete that, given his current health conditions.

I think in the interest of justice and mercy, looking at the fact that you are going to give him penalties with regards to each of these files, that 90 months as what's required by Minnesota Sentencing Guidelines would be a fair and just sentence in this regard. Thank you.... Your Honor. I failed to mention that, but with regards to the restitution that's been submitted to the Court for the amount of, I believe $2,383.57 –

THE COURT: Correct, to the Minnesota Department of - well, it's the Crime Victims Reparations Board.

DEFENSE ATTORNEY: We're in agreement that that figure is the accurate figure.

THE COURT: All right. Mr. Ross, is there anything you want to say on your own behalf?

THE DEFENDANT: I would like to address my family.

THE COURT: You may.

THE DEFENDANT: Tia, Ana, I can only pray that some-day that you will be able to forgive me for what I've done. Um, don't blame yourselves. This relies directly on my shoulders. I am to blame. I am fully to blame. You are not to blame in any way.

Um, I would also like to address my wife. Aren, I'm sorry for the pain that I've brought on this family. I made a promise to you 20 years ago that I would make your lives so happy. I have failed in that promise.

I would also like to say that there is $500 in the safe. You go ahead and use that if you need it. The key is on top of my dresser in the coffee can. If you need my van, you can have it. The title is in the top drawer of the desk. It's al-ready signed.

Please remove that old beat-up heater from my bedroom. The Vornado fan is in my van towards the very back. That's a safer heater.

I would also like you to get in touch with my attorney and get a quit claim deed started; I want to turn the house over to your name and your name only.

When I was in college, I learned of a program that whereby when one spouse goes to prison, the other spouse can receive payments through the Government. I can't remember who offers that, whether it be the Social Security Administration or whatever, you might have to look on the Internet to find who offers that or even if it's in existence any more.

I would also like to request that there are two CDs in the van between the two front seats in white CD sleeves, these are my novels that I've written, could you please send them to Joe. Aren, don't – don't blame yourself for the behavior I've done. I'm sorry for breaking up this family.

Kids, I'd like you to go home tonight and read Leviticus, Chapter 18, Verse 6, and then read Verses 29, and you will understand what is happening here.

Your Honor – Your Honor, that's all I have to say.

THE COURT: Mr. H. is back. Did you get 252 days?

MR. H.: Yes, I did.

THE COURT: All right. That's what my clerk checked on MINCIS calculator, and that's through yesterday.

DEFENSE ATTORNEY: And I would agree with that.

THE COURT: All right. Well, the Court has carefully considered the factors that apply in deciding whether or not a permissive concurrent or consecutive sentence should be imposed.

And the Court finds that all of the factors very much weigh in having consecutive sentences. And basically, um, some of them are outlined here.

The Court has not considered the position of authority because that – that was one of the factors in the sentence.

The Court has considered the size of the defendant and how intimidating that was, particularly that this was not a single act against each of these individuals, but many, many acts over a 10-year period, um, and starting at – as early as age 4, it would appear.

Particularly important here is that if the sentences does not run consecutively, you are getting absolutely no sentence for a second victim. And that would be just totally unfair.

For the single sentence, basically, it would be a 90-month sentence, seven and a half years. With good time that's only five years in prison for this conduct is just not reasonable at all.

So with respect to count seven, the Court does hereby commit you to the Commissioner of Corrections for a period of 90 months. And the Court is giving you credit for 252 days served through yesterday because your commitment starts running today.

The Court is imposing the mandatory minimum fine of $50, a $77 assessment, total $127, plus a $28 public defender co-pay. The total amount ordered is $155.

The Court is also ordering restitution to the Minnesota Crime Victim's Reparations Board in the sum of $2,383.57.

Now, this commitment is subject to a 5-year conditional release. That means whenever you are released on conditional release or supervised release. It will run for a period of 5 years from that date. And if you violate the conditions of your release, you could go back to prison potentially for that remaining five years.

The Court is also recommending sex offender treatment to the Commissioner.

For count eight, the court does hereby commit you to the Commissioner of Corrections for a period of 90 months, running consecutive with count seven.

The Court is not imposing any additional fines or assessments. And again, restitution is ordered as in count ones, and there's conditional – 5-year conditional release.

Do you have any questions?

THE DEFENDANT: No.

THE COURT: I'm going to have you sign each of these at the bottom. You will get the green copy.

But first, I want to advise you that if you are not happy with this sentence, you have a right to appeal it; you do that to the Minnesota Court of Appeals. If you're indigent, cannot afford a lawyer, the State Public Defender would represent you. Your attorney can advise you of the procedures for in. Plaintiff's attorney?

PLAINTIFF'S ATTORNEY: Your Honor, has the Court ordered that Mr. Ross register as a predatory offender and a DNA sample as well?

THE COURT: No. I — don't tear those off yet. Let me put that on. That's required by Statute, but I'll put it in there – put it in the order itself.

PLAINTIFF'S ATTORNEY: Thank you, Your Honor.

THE COURT: All right. You're remanded to the custody of the Sheriff for transfer to the Commissioner of Corrections.

STATE OF MINNESOTA (COUNTY NAMED)

I, [Court Reporter], do hereby certify that the foregoing transcript, consisting of the preceding pages, is a true and complete transcription of the audio recording of the proceedings to the best of my ability.

(Dated)

/s/

_________________________________ Official Court Reporter

****

CHAPTER 11
Healing With Therapy & Treatments

It has taken a lot of time for our family to go through treatment and healing. Several years have passed, and we are getting better and healthier than ever, thanks to the help of several types of professional therapy. Sometimes, we take two steps forward and one step backward in our healing struggles. The great news is when we need treatment again, we can always return! Families who experience the trauma of incest and child sexual abuse can benefit from working with counselors, therapists, psychologists, and psychiatrists. Talk therapy helped the three of us most.

One of my recent treatments included the use of palm vibrators. They were oval-shaped and vibrated back and forth in my palms while I talked about my happy memories with my daughters.

Favorite Things

This technique helps calm the mind and restore happy thoughts and feelings. My favorite ideas and activities include the following:

- Boat
- Books
- Church
- Computers

- Hot platter with buttered rice
- Nurturing, learning, curiosity, wonder, and creativity
- Spaghetti and meatballs
- Oatmeal raisin cookies
- Parks
- Thrift stores with the girls – enjoyed playing in the toy section
- Weekends to Southwest Minnesota for visits with grandparents
- Shopping (at Walmart, for example)

Facing Facts

The first thing our family did to begin healing from incest was to face the awful truth head-on. I highly recommend talk therapy. There was a lot of group counseling for the girls, but there was no women's support group for mothers or fathers of incest victims that the social workers or health care advocates could develop. My daughters and I had a few group sessions in counseling. The girls had several group sessions that included many other victims of incest. A family doctor tried to connect me with one other mom of the victims. The victim's mom never returned any of my phone calls. It's a shameful situation, and very few people want to talk about what happened.

Singles, couples and families, and groups can benefit from talk therapy. Medication is another option if needed. Individuals can benefit from spiritual guidance and support.

In 2008, a little more than a year had passed. I was a mental mess! I consulted with a Psychotherapist that was also a hypnotist. I happened to find him on a dating site. The Reparations Board covered my therapy sessions. The massage therapy chair was extremely uncomfortable for me since it squeezed my legs too tight, and the massage parts were rough on my back. I had to put a stop to that painful massage chair. I continued for a total of 10 sessions. The therapist made personalized tapes for me so I could listen to them. In one of the sessions, I admitted that I was eating baby food cereal for some reason. I intensely craved the taste! It continued for several more months. Then I stopped eating baby food cereal. In August, when I stopped going to therapy, the girls and I took the Greyhound Bus out to California for our vacation. We drove from Los Angeles to Pismo Beach in a rental van to spend several days enjoying the sand and huge waves of water.

My latest counselor (2020) suggested using a strategy called "Your Most Resourceful Self" (MRS) in my most recent talk therapy. I learned that I could let my workplace supervisor know that I felt stressed out and needed a few moments to gather my composure. I knew I had done the best thing when I told her I needed a break. I asked if she would call the medical team in the building if I had a severe panic attack. Many coworkers have not been able to express their feelings to her. I've seen many leave the company while others went to other departments. Others have taken the issues to her manager. That seems to get people nowhere since her manager believes that all the complainers pick on the supervisor. This supervisor can remember everything and makes employees feel as though they are five years old when she gets incredibly technical about every cleaning detail. The technique becomes more important than the outcome. Since I've approached her with my extreme frustrations, she has listened to me, and I will say, "so far, so good." I had to be bold, which works for me.

It can take years to recover from child sexual abuse. I have learned this since becoming aware of our family tragedy. My older daughter Tia has a darkness in her soul that she can't seem to escape. My Ana often has recurring nightmares. I hope a beautiful miracle happens where they can forever forget and leave behind the ball and chain that currently seems to hold them. A very well-meaning relative has told me to imagine them well. That sounds nice. I want that to happen!

Research is Needed

I believe people should research sexual abuse more often than they do. There is much to do to help children be safe by empowering them with the knowledge of protecting themselves. There also is a lot to discover in learning about how pedophiles work.

Since incest is taboo and not publicly discussed very often, I did not know much about it. I certainly was not expecting it to occur in my home. As soon as the family crime came to light, I began looking for answers to how and why it occurred. I hope someday to discuss why this happened with our daughters with my ex-husband. My daughters were victims. That left me troubled and grief-stricken. I wanted to know how this problem had developed and what my role might have been. I knew that I had never approved of such activity, so none of it was my fault. I consistently tried to protect them from predators throughout my children's young lives. I knew that sexual assault was a problem in schools and churches by hearing about it in the news. I felt that my husband and I were a team. I was expecting together, we could protect our children.

One tactic we tried to protect the girls was to homeschool them. But that works only if neither parent is a pedophile.

Following a year of paying for a high-priced private education for our older daughter, we switched to homeschooling. For the next several years, we used various curricula. By 2004, we got both girls a computer to support their schooling using many educational DVDs. They both loved digital art and looking up research (topics they were interested in) online.

Ironically, I spent considerable time studying how sexual assaults on children happen. I found very little information on how someone can spot a pedophile before tragedy strikes and the family is broken. I questioned what I could have done to protect the girls from being victimized. These criminals don't usually reveal their intentions. You think you know someone. Then you find out that you don't know that person at all. The abusers have ways to keep victims quiet, at least for a while. Eventually, I asked my daughter about her thoughts while going to a birthday party. She told me that her father had been secretly abusing her and her sister. I was shocked. "He was sneaky about it," she explained to me. That day was the last I would see him for years.

I learned that a parent could inform the child early in life that other people should not be touching their bodies and tell Mom or Dad if someone wants to do that. We can explain good touch and bad touch. Even well-meaning relatives and friends should let them be if they don't want to be hugged or kissed. If they are taught that their bodies are private and in their control, it could help defend them from pedophile damage. Children need to be trained on how to speak out about inappropriate behavior.

I am still learning about what causes this tragedy and ways to prevent it from happening. If I can learn from experts, I will gladly share the answers.

Parents must closely guard their children. Question everything! Children need knowledge and respect. They can get away from abuse by using their voices. They can know what self-respect is with the help of family.

Like other diseases and crimes, incest can be overcome and put in the past.

Encouragement for Teen Survivors of Sexual Abuse

Being a teenager, in some ways, resembles a pioneer's life. A young person approaching the legal age of eighteen begins to explore the world on their terms. Sometimes there are mysteries to figuring out the best thing to do in each situation. Everything may seem new and unfamiliar, and teens often worry that the wrong step could lead them into trouble.

When sexual abuse happens, many teens don't know what to do. They may lose trust in the adults who are responsible for them. They could suffer physical or emotional injuries but not know who to tell. They may experience fear, shame, guilt, and worry. It is crucial for a teen or preteen to turn to a trustworthy adult and seek advice, hopefully, a family member who responds respectfully and thoughtfully and can take the proper steps to provide help.

Encouragement for Moms/Dads of Sexually Abused Children

Those who have experienced sexually abused children will need to connect with people who can help them talk about what has happened to their children and what to do about the sexual abuse that their children have suffered. We can learn a great deal from experts, like counselors, pastors, psychologists, and those who have experienced similar types of abuse. They can teach us how to become wiser about protecting future generations from experiencing the tragedy of sexual abuse. We can also be on alert for those children around us who show signs of being sexually abused. Parents, guardians, and teachers must listen to what kids talk about and how they behave or look. Symptoms of abused children may include an attitude of distress or depression. They might wear provocative clothing or appear to suffer neglect by not eating well or wearing the proper dress. Some victims may exhibit injuries or make emotional statements referencing the abuse.

Find Freedom from the Past

It sometimes takes a while to pick up the pieces after a tragic event.

Tia and Ana were understandably free! Their abuser was incarcerated now. They would never have to see him again. Although they were laughing and happy, I cried out loud because of the tragedy. I couldn't hold it in. I couldn't cover up my emotions. I felt how greatly my children were cheated out of their innocent childhoods. They were forced to bear years of abuse. I was missing the remarkable man I thought had loved us all. My children were not ready to talk to me about what had happened to them at the time. I know that their father trained them to be silent about their abuse.

I was free, too, of my former husband's occasional quirkiness. I had no significant other to disagree with me. I started making my own decisions on everything now. I was free of caring for an abrasive significant other. I began to enjoy the adventure of finding a brand-new love.

Starting Over

I decided to start life anew by dusting myself off and picking up the pieces.

I watched my girls regarding how they were coping. It seemed like we were each recovering individually by participating in talk therapy. We made some strides by changing the inside of the house. I wish I could have moved us to a tropical island so we could really forget about it all and escape that life forever! The girls begged me to move away, but I felt I couldn't afford it.

The next best thing was to remove much of the house's collected junk. We also made our own spaces the way we wanted them. My Tia painted her room a light peach color and used the queen bed that her dad once had, minus the bed frame. She also put down a different rug. She and I went to the thrift store to pick up a desk for $5 for her room.

My Ana decided to paint her room also. The east wall was black, and the other three sides were light fluorescent green. At her request, I changed the bare wooden floor to carpet. She chose a light, dull green color. I also got her a new full-size bed.

My room was still upstairs. I didn't feel the need to change much physically. I was looking to fill my void with a good husband.

Soon, the girls started going to church again with encouragement from their friends around town. The church pastors were like fathers to them. Several boys and a small number of girls attended that church. My daughters would often hang out at the church with the youth group. Sometimes while I was at work, they would come to my house. Sometimes I would go home to find broken windows or other mischief evidence.

During this transition phase, I often spent time crying and wanting very badly to escape this miserable life by going for walks through town in the middle of the quiet night on my days off. I spent many days out in the park preserves in the area. Nature helped me get away from the nightmare of losing the excellent companion I thought I once had - and the chaos he caused. On rare occasions, my girls and I would take walks around the town to spend time outdoors in good weather, enjoying each other's company and conversations about whatever was on our minds.

A short time later, I decided to start attending the church my girls were going to. I was relieved watching them develop healthy teen lives. Thankfully, I witnessed them making close, much-needed friendships.

My older daughter Tia was 16 when she got hired at the Labrador retriever kennel owned by two veterinarians that lived out in the country. Ana started the following year. With their own money, they could buy the clothes they wanted. I took care of our living expenses, like the grocery bill ranging from $150 to $200 per week. I worked overtime, and we ate well. The girls chose their favorite high-priced juices, vegetables, and expensive meat cuts. The three of us became a reliable team working together to move forward.

I drove Tia or Ana to the kennel to work for three to four hours per day, one daughter went every other day, and the other daughter worked the remaining days. Tia loved dogs, so she enjoyed her work, but Ana did not care much for the job. It was a lovely country farm. Dr. J. and Dr. F. owned and ran a Veterinarian Hospital in the big city. Beautiful black, large and tall Percheron horses stood in the pasture. They also raised several litters of pedigree Labrador Retrievers, selling them for about $1,500 each. The vet couple had a large Macaw that lived inside their house in the winter and an enormous outdoor terrarium during the warm months. When the many dogs in the kennel barked, the Macaw would yell, "Quiet!" It brought happy humor into my shattered world.

My girls also babysat for a few children in the area. They were ambitious. I was very proud of them. My highly energetic younger Ana eventually worked at Taco Bell, providing excellent customer service. Her older sister was somewhat laid back in her ways. Tia worked happily for a cleaning service. Ana was eventually placed in charge of many employees in an un-named company with several thousand employees, making a better living than me.

I am grateful for my mom and sister, who stayed with me on the phone while crying and worked to get the family chaos back in order. Sometimes my mom would ask about Daniel in prison, "I wonder how he feels?" My mom would have empathy for the vilest people. She had a heart for all. I just let her talk and wonder. I was sad and curious too.

I was under a great deal of stress. Dad scolded me for the way my hair looked. I was losing it. I exclaimed that I was sorry that it had happened. My life was a mess! People at work gave me hassle about my hair too. My hair is very fine and dry. Perhaps some of it is inherited from one of my great-grandmas, who somehow stuffed the hair from her brush back into her hair by wrapping it in.

I should have insisted on one thing! My Ana and I should have found better things to do than be with boyfriends. I failed her. It was a wild goose chase for me to find someone to keep. Clearly, I did wrong by letting her spend lots of time with her boyfriend while hunting down my God-fearing husband-to-be, which I felt I deserved.

Looking for Love

During the summer of 2007, I got acquainted with a disabled physician friend I found on a dating site. This time I was determined to find someone successful like a doctor. I was gradually learning that he was struggling with alcoholism. He had a solid commitment to his extended family. He financially supported his sister, her buff, carpet laying, husband, and four children. I grew attached to him since I aimed to fill that void in my life.

My husband was incarcerated, waiting for trial. I began dating before I divorced my husband of 20- plus years. I met Denny on a Christian dating site. He was a real chap-wearing cowboy, a widower 19 years older than me from Ohio. I visited him on PTO during the week of my 48th birthday. He had an arena for horses and cattle where contests were held, and he belonged to the Ohio Cutting Horse Association. I enjoyed my time riding in the horse arena and the company of other horse lovers. I helped him with housekeeping and tilled his garden. He and I went for a ride on his Harley around the southern tip of Lake Erie. I hadn't been on a motorcycle ride for over 30 years! We also went to see Edison Woods Reserve. It was a remarkable escape from reality for a few days. After my fantastic vacation days were over, I returned to work and my family. We continued to communicate by phone. I wanted to meet with him on another PTO. He then let me know about the new love he had found.

She was a local lady who was a horse-riding instructor, and they ultimately married. They complimented each other career-wise.

My divorce was finalized a few days after my Ohio adventure.

Daniel was a widower and retired postal worker. He was 17 years older than me. It concerned him somewhat that his name was the same as my ex's. He and his talkative, platonic girlfriend drove over to see me one day. "What? How strange," I thought to myself. It was awkward. Then we all walked around Murphy Hanrahan Park. I liked that he practiced his faith, but he was looking for a clue that we were to be together - if he got a Christmas card from me (he told me later), it was a sure sign that we were to be a couple. His lovely wife, who had died of cancer, had been a consistent card sender for Christmas, but I wasn't into that, so we went our separate ways.

Not long after that, I met a truck-driving former chiropractor who lost his job due to an accident. Pete was ten years older than me. He was recently unemployed when I met him and a Bible Scholar, and very intelligent. He belonged to a long-distance on-line church called Faithful Church of God in Laodicea, where the pastor lives in Malta. His wife had wanted the divorce. He was a father of three boys and one girl. He proposed marriage a few days after we met, and we went to the courthouse to apply for a marriage license. We stayed together for a little over five years. He helped me with a few projects around the house and yard. We attended church together regularly. But he had a fascination for Asian women and communicated with one, which I discovered while searching the internet on my computer.

I informed my elder daughter Tia about what I had found. She told him off through Facebook and shamed him out of our lives. On the last day I would ever see him, I came home from my night job, and the dryer was running. On the kitchen table was some chocolate. I saw that he had shuffled around dishes in the cupboard. Some of our items were gone. I noticed that he left behind much of his property. Yet, I decided that I was going to be okay. My friends at the Loaves and Fishes Dinners asked me what had happened to Pete. They listened in their sweet, caring way. They told me that I deserved much better than how he treated me. I felt comforted by their condolences.

Soon, I decided to look for an engineer. I found one about five miles away from my home. He had lost his beautiful wife a few years earlier from diabetes complications. He was an excellent conversationalist. We enjoyed many hours of home-cooked meals that he made more often than I did. We played Yahtzee almost every day, and on occasion, we played Sequence. I was a substitute teacher in more than 50 different area schools during that time. I met many other teachers, parents, and inspiring students. This retired manufacturing engineer had a couple of sons he was devoted to raising years before. I never saw his sons or any of his grandchildren for all those nine months that we were together. He would talk about them and their impressive accomplishments but seem snappy at most everyone except me and the people in the church we attended together. I loved going to church with him and joined the handbell choir. We made Norwegian Lefse at the church around Thanksgiving for the church's youth activities fundraiser. The St. James Quilters also made many beautiful quilts for sale draped over several pews.

My engineer friend shared his basement with a lady renter that took care of some house bills. He had a devoted younger brother who would often stop by his house to see how he was doing. Other siblings, he talked to by phone. He survived a heart operation about a year before his wife died. The doctor gave him a 25 percent chance of making it due to his life-long addictions to chain drinking and smoking. After drinking, he would sleep for hours. The habit was killing him. I learned from a physician friend who was an alcoholic that alcohol addiction is like a craving for water. I studied a small book on alcoholism long before meeting him since I grew up with no alcoholism in our immediate family.

The lady that lived in the basement and I would either hide his alcohol or dump it. I took him to the hospital when needed and drove him to doctor appointments. His brother and I were by his bedside when he died. His family did not even acknowledge that I was his close companion in his obituary. I felt terrible at the time but soon realized I would be just fine.

Two days after my companion's funeral, a stalker approached me in one of my frequented libraries. He asked, "Aren't you lonely; don't you want company? "

I saw that he was about half my age, and I wanted someone my age. Whenever he tried to converse with me, I politely said that I had someone in my life, even though I only imagined a relationship with someone my age. He approached me several times until I showed him a gentleman friend's picture about my age. I haven't seen him since that.

I learned how to text messages from a North Dakota man, 4 hours away, whom I met on a dating site. I took a vacation there around Hillsboro, where I found a motel. I sent text messages to meet him at one of the restaurants, but he never showed up. So, I enjoyed a nice, quiet vacation just waiting around for no one in particular and making small talk with the locals, walking around the small town.

My next love was 6'5" Lars, a widower that lost his wife about nine years before I met him. He was not a heavy drinker but got pulled over by a cop. His blood-alcohol level was barely over the limit. He had to spend some time in jail. Then he was on house arrest. We spent time walking at a local state park every weekend. We went out to eat at Applebee's every Saturday evening.

I thought we were in love with each other, but I eventually learned that I was the only one with that thought. He only talked about marriage a couple of times. I was hopeful. I should have picked up on the clues that he wouldn't get married. He regularly spoke to other women on the phone while I was with him. Soon he was going places with a lady 12 years older than he was. She had a boyfriend, he told me. She was not interested in a relationship with him. I decided to look for someone interested in staying together.

I found a "Christian man" in the Craigslist dating section. The preacher/cop lived about 2 hours away on a farm. He had been a cop for around 18 years in Wisconsin. He worked for an auto parts store and was a part-time preacher. He had a beautiful Chesapeake Labrador. I was very much in love with his cheerful, loyal, ball-catching tan Lab. Preacher Man was very nice, with a unique sense of humor. I enjoyed our many drives around the countryside and the state parks in Minnesota and Wisconsin. I was in shape. He complimented me on that. He is knowledgeable about endless subjects. You name it. He knows it! He let me borrow some of his books to read.

His money management skills were a bit problematic to me. I definitely would have needed separate bank accounts. We would have to live in a duplex if we were going to be together. He was looking for someone special in his life, someone to marry.

When we were dating, he planned a move to Wyoming to preach. I'm very proud his dream job came his way. Another reason why I could not go is that I could not leave my grandson behind. I have kept in touch with PC. I have not dated for almost three years. Joining a dance club was helpful until the pandemic separated me from my dance partners. One of these days, I'm going to get back to it!

I have had a crush for almost three years now. Someone close to my age. It probably won't go anywhere because the Ken doll I am interested in doesn't feel secure with relationships. I can read him like a book. I enjoy chatting with him and teasing him until he flops his hand like he's saying, "nonsense." I give him compliments, but he doesn't seem to believe me. Then I run off to work on my nine-to-five job, where he visits every day.

Spiritual Healing: "Look to Me – I AM the Answer!"
While I was walking at a park by Union Lake, I heard a message that came to my thoughts,

"Look to Me – I AM the Answer!"

I believed it! But I also wanted a man I could hug, talk to, and touch.

I kept the message in mind and heard it over and over again. Yet, I still wanted a man's physical presence, frantically searching for the human that would stay with me in a loving, committed relationship. He would see that I was worthy of being loved. I met numerous gentlemen, but I was selective, or they were not looking for a permanent relationship.

My quest to find a loving man continued for years. I am not sorry it ended. Or maybe it hasn't ended. But I am not going to work anymore at it. I am now content to be loved by someone supernatural who will always love me perfectly. Is there anyone better than that?

Jesus is my answer! I would still welcome a human companion, but I believe I have finally given up for good. I am at peace. My void has been filled, knowing that Jesus loves me unconditionally. Life is good.

CHAPTER 12
Advocates for the Abused

All those who care and are concerned for children's sexual safety should understand how to become their advocates. The child will be helped with quick action to protect them.

Child Protective Services in the United States are aware of the problem and openly address this subject in employee training workshops and public service presentations. The department is often part of a larger social services organization that oversees poverty relief and child well-being for kids in families at risk or in trouble. However, they cannot take action until they receive adequate and accurate information about the children who may be victims of sexual abuse. These agencies may require a family's medical or legal referral for assistance. Child Protective Services | Childcare.gov says on their website:"If you suspect that a child is being abused or neglected, or if you are a child that is mistreated, call 1-800-422-4453 immediately. (www.childhelp.org) This Child Help National Child Abuse Hotline is available 24 hours a day, seven days a week. The hotline can provide information on how to make a report."

Child Advocacy Centers (CACs) are local programs established to help abused children by coordinating an investigation of alleged child sexual abuse. They offer abused kids and their families long-term advocacy and, if needed, healthcare. These organizations facilitate children's treatment as sex abuse victims by networking with local law enforcement, judicial, social services, and medical entities. (www.nationalcac.org)

Children's relatives and friends must watch for ways to protect kids from a very early age, even infants. Although most people generally know that children should not be viewed or treated as sexual objects, some family members do not maintain healthy boundaries, primarily if they are influenced by drugs or alcohol. Other perpetrators may have diagnosed or undiagnosed mental health issues. They need healthy adults to inform them of acceptable versus unacceptable interactions with children of all ages. Watch for questionable behaviors when they spend time around young children.

I highly recommend the following websites and video presentations that talk to children about how to prevent or stop any abuse:

www.FightChildAbuse.org

Videos for grades K-3, 4-6, and Teens

www.YouTube.com

Search for

- *Good Touch and Bad Touch* by Atul Tyagi Wow Kids

- *My Body Safety Rules - 5 Things Every Child Should Know* by Educate2Empower Publishing

- *My Body Belongs to Me From My Head to My Toes*

You can easily find the sources using any search engine.

Parents should also pay attention to what small children are drawing. Ask questions about the drawing:

- Who is that?

- What are they doing?

- Where is this place?

- What is happening?

Asking all kinds of questions could lead to a revelation. If I had asked my daughter specific questions about the "monster" drawing that she drew in the stairwell as a preschooler, as depicted on and inside this book cover, perhaps things would have turned out another way.

Parents should also ask about any unusual dreams that small children mention. One day in the car, it struck me as peculiar when I heard young Tia say, "I had a dream that a man poked a hole in my wee-wee." I don't think that young children can sometimes distinguish between a dream and reality. I didn't have any proof that it could have been her dad touching her, and it didn't seem likely that he or anyone we knew was hurting my daughter in that way. I've been reminding myself to question everything!

Moms and dads, grandparents, and extended family members need to be willing to train children early to know what they can do to speak up for themselves regarding inappropriate touch, talk, or other forms of contact. Schools, libraries, and family-centered social service agencies often have books, videos, and other resources to inform families so they can avoid or identify this problem.

People affiliated with church-based support groups could be asked to work out a watch plan. Child victims and their families may feel it would be beneficial to participate in a support group.

All people who work around children need to be watchful and proactive to protect our family's and communities' young, innocent lives.

It would be interesting to start a conversation with those who can tell their stories about how they managed to stop sexual abuse from getting started. It would help to know how they discovered the risk and prevented it before things went too far. Sometimes I try to imagine how our family might have been if I had told my children what they could and should say to avoid "bad touch" if anyone touched them inappropriately.

There are now also age-specific children's books about the subject of inappropriate touch. When my girls were young, I would have bought such a book to prevent their dad, who I depended on to keep them safe in all ways, from inflicting his terrible damage on them.

I believe knowledge and teamwork are weapons for preventing children at risk of sexual abuse. Now that I've gotten a bit wiser about sexual abusers and their victims, I would like to share what I've learned in hopes that it will help other families dealing with this problem. Families and individuals without child sexual abuse problems can better understand the nature of this sexual deviance.

Teach Children How to Communicate About Abuse

- Children must know who they can trust.

- Sexual predators confuse children.

- Kids must get every chance to tell a parent, a caregiver, a teacher, or a trustworthy authority about any concerns or fears.

- Teach your children how to express certain emotions or concerns in ways you can understand. This teaching will enable them to inform you if a pedophile says or does something inappropriate to them.

- Avoid keeping children isolated by being too busy to listen to them. They need to know that they will be treated with the highest level of respect they deserve where they thrive the best.

- Teach them to respect their bodies and tell you (or another trusted authority) if someone tries to touch them improperly.

- They need to be guided on what they can do if they become trapped in such a situation. Family members can team up to work together to protect children from abuse.

- Secrets should be discouraged. They should learn to trust you and tell you about everything that happens to them. Children should be allowed to say whatever is on their minds and know that you will listen respectfully and respond fairly.

How Should We Respond to Pedophiles?

I learned from my ex that pedophiles get beaten up in prison. An occasional person seen in the news will kill a child molester with no regrets. "South Carolina Couple Admits to Killing Sex Offender, wife." (YouTube, May 29, 2014) I would much prefer to send them anywhere in outer space. They could have a one-way ticket. You could keep yourself out of prison that way! I had felt like killing my ex while Ana was suffering in the hospital because of the abuse. If I had, I would not have gotten the chance to see my daughters grow up or hold my adorable grandson. There can be other solutions. Give your children a verbal black-belt to defend themselves. Always watch and secure your children. There are sex offender registries to know where the offenders are. Stay away from those locations!

Question Everything: Indicators of Pedophile Behavior

Many predators put up such an excellent front to spouses and family members that their children's sexual abuse is never suspected. I believe the abuse continued for so long in my house because I never questioned my spouse. It was a given, a shared value and marriage goal, that we would take good care of our children. He was interested in keeping them safe, too, or so I thought. Since we were raising our biological offspring together in a harmonious, happy household, I did not sense any warning signs about his behavior toward the children, at least not at first.

There was a time when we were working on a meal together. Dan described a guy our babysitter's friends had brought to the church. He stated, "I think that guy is a pedophile."

My quick response was, "Well, let's keep the girls away from him!"

It puzzled me why he would mention that to me. I have learned that those with pedophile behavior are incredibly secretive and clever in controlling their victims through love, fear, or anxiety. He told the children that authorities would come and take him away to jail. They had to be secretive about whatever he did to them. He did not threaten them in any other way. Their feelings were manipulated by their father. They were dealing with a narcissist! They loved and aimed to please their father. They wanted to protect their family life. They kept his sexual abuse a secret.

I learned this from the girls about their dad's manipulation of them:

- Their dad never threatened their lives.

- He instilled in them fear and guilt.

- He warned them that they would be taken away to a family that didn't love them.

- He told them how horrible foster care was and that they were safer with him.

- He threatened them with what Children's Protective

Services would do and what they would ask; "He instructed us to lie to them if they ever took us away."

- He began conditioning the girls with these warnings and threats when Tia was four, and Ana would have been about two.

My Tia explained that her dad was sneaky about his behavior. She informed me of the issue when we left for a birthday party, and that was the last we ever saw him at home.

"Why didn't I see what was going on?" I asked, bewildered and horrified.

Since then, I've learned that there are clues to tell from reading and research. It is important to note if someone wants to expose their body unnaturally. Parents and other adults should keep their bodies covered with appropriate dress.

Another clue is when children are talked to in ways meant only for adult ears. Treating children as adults is a red flag, especially concerning sex-related topics.

We must inform children at a very young age to communicate if they are being touched inappropriately. They should learn early in life that no one has the right to touch their private areas.

I believe if I had told Tia and Ana how to protect themselves, the situation might have turned out another way. Children need to be aware from a very young age to reveal any unusual or disturbing treatment from others, including other children or teens, and adults.

Adults must take it upon themselves to always watch over the children in their care.

Pedophiles are clever at getting jobs where young, vulnerable children are found, such as in daycare centers, schools, and playgrounds. They also pry their way into the lives of lonely, desperate women or men who want a companion without looking at their character as closely as they should. It's quite a challenge to catch a pedophile before they do any damage.

"How to Spot and Stop a Pedophile" (Chrissy B Show, June 2, 2017). I found some great information to consider in this YouTube video. Be observant. Notice if something is abnormal, like lap-sitting where the child is on the abuser's private parts with clothes or wrestling games. The abuser manipulates the child by talking in a whisper or alone. If a young child under the age of seven talks in detail about what has happened to them. It is probably likely that they have been sexually abused.

More awareness is necessary to protect children from sexual predators, especially those in their own families. Research, education, and discussion could bring experts and families together to learn more about this problem. We can take proactive steps to combat this problem and protect children from its harm as a community.

Being silent about such a devastating epidemic is not a solution. We must communicate clearly and effectively, asking questions as often as needed until we find answers and solutions.

Pedophiles know how much they are hated and despised. Often, they will not seek help but withdraw into silence and possibly denial until they inevitably hurt a child or adolescent. Feeling cut off from mainstream society and everyday life, they dwell on their distorted fantasies without getting the help they need.

CHAPTER 14
Newfound Freedoms

After their dad was gone, my daughters were often giggling and happy. They ran inside the house and out and about with friends or each other in our small city. I now understand why they felt relieved and free!

I have studied many online sources to learn about child sexual abuse. On the one hand, the more I learned, the worse I felt, experiencing waves of great sadness and loneliness as the pieces of my daughters' childhood trauma began to form a horrible picture that was extremely difficult to face. On the other hand, it made sense why the girls became ecstatic and lively when there wasn't an overly controlling, highly demanding father to order them around senselessly. They had survived the awful trauma for over a decade by that monster father, whom I had been clueless.

Over time, I have tried to talk to them to understand better what happened and how it happened. My Tia and Ana have displayed anger and frustration in my quest for answers, and I eventually understood.

I would sit down in front of the TV to watch *"To Catch a Predator"* with Chris Hansen as the interviewer of many who wanted to get to know some young person they met online. I was so intrigued and so puzzled about what made them tick. Why?

A detective solved one of my questions. He said that they aren't wired right.

Sometime later, I figured out that my daughters were programmed not to talk to me about the details of what happened between them and their father. When I was looking for Mr. Right, I hoped to find an amazing dad for the kids I could trust to help raise our children in a Godly, happy home. That had been my goal since young adulthood. Hopes for a healthy family were shattered. That week of January 10, 2007, changed our family for good! My Ana went by ambulance to the Mayo Clinic Teen Suicide Center.

A few months after SWAT removed their father from our home, my Tia, at the age of 16, asked me an unusual question, "Mom? Is it okay to think that sex is icky? " It took me by surprise. I said that whatever she thought was okay.

While I was at work, the girls continued to host numerous parties at our house. Many teens from the church youth group of the local Assemblies of God Church came over to share whatever fun they created! Other teens in town also came over to share the joy as well. Our place was a favorite hangout, but a few parents urged their teens not to go. I would go home to find a messy house and occasional broken and destroyed items.

Then I discovered several items had disappeared, like cash and many of my imprisoned husband's possessions. For a mom of teens on their own without supervision, I was patient and understanding, believing everything would work out in time if I gave my girls and their friends a chance to grow up and become more responsible.

There was a time when the girls went out with a friend, JoAnna, who went speeding through town. The police stopped her and brought my girls home to our front door. I let the girls in, and the police officer explained what had happened. I saw by their facial expressions that the event had been totally out of their control. I believed them. Though I am biased, they have been good girls considering what they have endured.

Ana enjoys life with her sister and friends and has a successful career. Ana got an Order For Protection since she was the only one of the three of us that applied for it. She's pretty happy and enjoys dining at classy restaurants with many friends.

Later, as I researched the effects and signs of child sexual abuse, I began understanding why my daughters celebrated as winter melted away and spring sprang! My diligent research on the internet also helped me understand why I cried before falling asleep every night. There was so much information to learn and know!

It is easy to misunderstand children's behavior when it changes to become unusual or inexplicable. My daughters became more outgoing. They tested their boundaries due to entering their teen years. Their abuse had kept them imprisoned for years in silent suffering. They were innocent children, forced to keep secrets from me and others who could have helped them. Finally, when the abuse ended, they embraced their newfound freedom wholeheartedly. They perhaps went overboard at times. They had to compensate for the loss of childhood they had experienced at the hands of the monster, who should have done everything possible to protect them.

It was not easy for me to watch them grow up and learn some difficult lessons. But it was far more tolerable to accept their behavior after discovering the abuse they had experienced in silence for years.

My older daughter Tia stayed out past curfew the night before turning 18. I saw it when she tested the police officer who reported the issue. The police talked about all the problematic behaviors the girls could get into when the family abuse came to light. It's what the officer told me he had learned about abused girls. Domestic abuse children often get into trouble, which I learned by reading relevant sources.

Tia was a prankster teasing the church youth pastor along with other friends. She enjoyed a good time doing silly, fun tricks that were unusual but not criminal or immoral. Nobody was ever hurt, just pranked! The church youth pastor tried to teach the teen boys and girls the Bible and important lessons about life. But the teens turned the weekly sessions into more of a church dating service. Of course, this was not the youth pastor's goal. The teens had to get set straight.

One of Tia's pranks was to open the house windows wide in January and turn up the heat! Oh my! I would get upset and complain! Yet I still believed her behavior would improve as she got older and more mature. I would explain to her that the heating bill was high. I was almost sure the town was warmer outside because of it! It seemed at least by one degree when I compared other nearby cities on the weather map.

I have kept in touch with the Youth Pastor throughout the years. He and the Senior Pastor would involve the girls in many ministries and activities. They held weekly Bible studies and encouraged the kids to pray and make wise decisions. Our Youth Pastor says, "Tia would frequently steal my mints from my desk and leave taunting notes from "the janitor". I remember her teasing our cat with a piece of popcorn and getting her finger sliced open." She would also take gum from the Youth Pastor's desk! One time the teens sprayed him with silly string! He kept the teens in line by involving them in worthwhile mission trips that were primarily local and rarely far away. They spent a few days at Pine Ridge Indian Reservation, helping the South Dakota Natives with anything they needed help with. It was a 12-hour drive. They took a couple of vans to get there.

They spent many days with their Valley Fair Season Passes riding roller coasters and going to other amusement park activities for several summers. They developed very close, lifelong friendships. They stayed busy in wholesome activities that helped them grow up healthy and moral. Those devoted pastors blessed my girls!! I am forever grateful for their help. The youth Pastor has been actively praying for my oldest daughter since she doesn't feel any connection with God, Jesus, or the Holy Spirit. Please say a quick prayer as you are reading this. "Please, Almighty God! Help Tia see how real you are and how much you love her! I want to see her in heaven where she won't have to be with murderers and rapists since You, God, can do anything!" "Save her soul!"

CHAPTER 15
The Almost Forgotten Voice

November 2012

Dear Aren,

It's been almost six years of not seeing or hearing from you, so I thought I'd break the silence. I think of you often. You don't live with somebody twenty years and forget them that easily.

If you write and tell me not to write anymore, I will understand, but I hope you won't do that.

Every day you are in my prayers when I thank God for Jesus Christ, salvation, the Holy Spirit, the Bible, my two daughters, and Aren.

I hope you voted.

Can you ever forgive me for the hurt I've placed on you? You always said to forgive was easy, but forgetting was hard. I left you to raise two teenagers on your own. Of course, Tia and Ana were pretty independent at that time. Thank God. Your financial burden, however, must have been heavy.

Try to focus on the good times. Remember when both of

us worked for security? What was the name of that really dark place in the Cities?

Believe it or not, I still dream of the old grainery, that I'm still working there. Those were tough days for us. Tia was almost born there. Ana was almost born in the car, on the way to some hospital in Minneapolis. I wonder if they know those stories.

I wrote a notebook and called it "Memories of Tia and Ana." In it, I wrote about the things the kids said and did and the times we shared.

One of Tia's early words was Hippopotamus. I put that in there. And when Ana would meet somebody new, she would say, "Hi, I'm Ana. She was so friendly even in those days. Remember the two blue horses she constantly carried around?

I sent the notebook to Tia for safekeeping. They have me moving around so much I didn't want it to get lost or stolen.

You should read it next time you see her. There's a lot of good memories in it.

Well, I can't begin to tell you how messed up this place is. But maybe that's what I deserve. These young men will start a fight at the drop of a hat. When I was at Appleton, that place was extremely violent. It was all I could do to avoid the madness.

One time, two rival gangs went at it in the gym. The only guard present was a tiny little young woman. Guys formed a battle line around her to protect her. I thought that was so neat. I wasn't there, I heard about it.

There was a family of rabbits outside my window last summer. It was fun to watch them grow up. The guards caught them all and removed them. It was a good thing because there was also a family of Bald Eagles in the bell tower. It was fun watching them grow up, too, learning how to fly. Man, they are as big as battleships now.

When I first got here, they took away my asthma inhaler. They said, "We don't want to pay for it." Joe (his brother) made a stink about it, so their story changed to, "You don't have asthma." Funny, the Mayo Clinic was wrong, and they were right? I've had asthma since 1961. Then, faced with overwhelming evidence, their story changed again to, "It's an allergic reaction." Well, allergic reaction or not, the fact still remains, "I can't breathe." So, I've been suffering with asthma attacks for two years. I find that drinking massive amounts of coffee helps, but it's not good for my heart.

How's Al at work these days? I remember I got a daily report about him a few years ago. Sometimes the way you talked, I thought he was the antichrist. I was always a good listener. After words, I would try to suggest alternatives, but I think it was better to let you vent your frustrations.

That's what I try to tell my young friends in here when they complain about their women. They say, "I don't like it when they tell me their troubles." Or "I don't like it when they complain to me." I tell them who else are they going to complain to other then their spouse. That's your job. If you want them to act like men, then marry a man. (You can do that in Iowa now-that's sick)

Well, I'm doing floors again just like I did for the old grocery store, stripping, waxing, and maintaining floor. I only get a dollar an hour, though. Tia says she's doing the same thing. I guess her early training working with me paid off.

I've broken my toe, and I'm on medical restriction. That means I can't work until it heals. My boss has assured me my job will be waiting for me when I get back. I don't know when it happened or even how it happened. I can't feel my feet. They were treating me for an infection. When it wasn't getting better, they x-rayed it and found that it was broken.

It's been five weeks now. I lost my job. I have no money coming in. Although my boss says as soon as I can go to work, she'd hire me back. That was nice of her.

She kinda reminds me of you. Same color hair, same eyes, and the same energy level. I just hope I don't lose my single cell because I lost my job. I labored long and hard to get a single cell. I didn't get into any trouble. I haven't been in any fights lately.

I've had a lot of time to think of things in here. I've come up with nine patentable inventions.

When I was a tutor in education, I learned how to patent an idea. I intend to do that once I get out. Like someone said, you don't have to have everybody buy one. You just need a million people to think it's a good idea.

Remember your solar-powered business card idea? Too bad it needed so much energy. The technology didn't exist back then, but now, solar power has come a long way, it might be possible. And the components needed have become so cheap. Keep that idea in mind.

First, you need to record the approximate date you thought of it. Then draw a sketch of it. Then get two friends to witness it and sign the drawing. Then make a patent search. Then fill out the paperwork to register it. It's just that easy. And there are attorneys that do nothing but search patent archives. (A scrolling marquee would really be eye-catching)

As I'm typing this letter, I'm reminded of when you taught me to line up the corners of the paper before I type.

I've written two books since I've been here. I don't know if I have a prayer of publishing them, though. But it's a hobby. I enjoy it. I wish I had my toon town books from home. I'd start editing them.

Tia said she was going to come visit me, but with her work schedule, I can't see how that's possible. She's working two jobs just to support that grandson. I respect her for that.

I haven't talked to Ana in a while. She's always sleeping when I call. There's so many things I want to say, but I don't want to bore you with a lengthy letter.

I hope you write me back. I know we can't be married, but

I hope we can be friends. I didn't know how you felt about me. I still don't.

Is the economy really as bad as they say it is? Tia says gas is almost $4 a gallon. That's your Dems for you. The president hasn't explored any new sources of oil. And that Canadian pipeline, why did he shoot that down? That would have given this economy a huge shot in the arm.

I'm writing this letter on Monday. Tomorrow's Tuesday, election day. I hope Romney wins. By the time you get this letter, we might have a new president. I don't think the president knows what he's doing.

Well, I think I'll end this letter. I don't mind telling you I'm rather apprehensive on how it will be received. I hope you've forgiven me after all these years and write me back.

Sincerely,

Dan

I didn't respond to the letter. I had nothing good to say, and I felt numb. I wasn't motivated to answer back. Nothing was required of me at the time. Returning his belongings was not necessary then.

January 1, 2017
Dear Aren,

You know what?

I'm a piece of sh**. When I was married to you, I stunk because I never took a bath. I was selfish, always getting my way, not to mention how I treated the girls, and when the tornado hit, I was the first one in the storm cellar instead of making sure the woman I loved was safe.

It's not hard to see why you hate me. Sometimes I think I would have served as much purpose as if I hadn't been born at all.

I don't have the right to ask you for anything: but I need my birth certificate and social security card.

My birth certificate was in a file named "IMPORTANT" in the file desk drawer, and my social security card was in the middle desk drawer inside my passport. Do not send my passport.

I'm out in 51 days. I'll be on ISR intensive supervised release (which is set up for failure).

Write back if you want to, even if you have to vent.

Please send my ID's.

Thank you.

Sincerely,

Dan

I was feeling anxious, not quite knowing what to do. I made attempts to avoid Dan. I tried to apply in one county for an Order For Protection, and OFP counselors denied it. I tried to apply for an OFP in another county and was denied. The girls rightfully got their OFP. I had to face the one who destroyed the girl's childhood to return his court-ordered items: clothes, albums, and coin collection.

April 30, 2018
Dear Aren,

Thank you for the list of stuff you sent me. I appreciate the fact that I can abandon any or all my stuff there.

In your opinion, how big of a truck would I need if I decided to take all of it?'

It is very important I get my heirlooms. And please, please, please, I need my external hard drive. Tia told me back in '09, she was taking some of my things to her house for safekeeping. I'm not asking you to contact her for me, just mentioning where my things might be.

Thank you very much for keeping my stuff. I am disappointed you won't be there on the 27th. It was very courteous of you to tell me that I may need a face mask.

Sincerely, ▪(You taught me to spell this word)

Dan

I still felt numb. Wishing it all to go away would be a miracle.

Editors note: These letters have been reproduced exactly as written. Spelling and grammatical errors included.

CHAPTER 16
Memories of Tia and Ana
Written in Prison

These memories have been shared with permission and encouragement from their father.

Me: I've been reading the memories you wrote again and again. We had such sweet, smart, beautiful little girls. I wish we could do it all over again as great, appropriately close parents.

Dan: Yes, I wish I could do it all over again too.

Me: Those were good memories; can I share them?

Dan: Yes.

Me: These are such vivid memories in this notebook.

Dan: I wrote that over the ten years I was sitting in prison.

Me: Nice use of prison time.

Dan: I missed them so ungodly bad.

Me: Did any other dads do that, writing memories?

Dan: I didn't want to lose those memories, so I thought I'd better write them down. Not that I know of. I'm glad you are enjoying them.

Me: Very nice part of your parenting. That part was awesome. Were there any other dads in prison that would talk to you about their kids?

Dan: I tried. I just had to have a flaw.

Me: Seriously, I have a set of flaws, too, that God and other people see.

Dan: No, I think you are the closest thing to perfect that can be.

Me: I appreciate that you think so well of me, yet I clearly am in the same flaw boat that you are.

For all of my faults, I did so love my kids. My love was genuine. I showed it in our everyday activities. Some of which are in this book. I would have killed to protect them. I would have died so they might live. Loyalty to family is my number one priority. I don't know if my family will ever enjoy this book. But maybe when I'm dead, by the Grace of God, they will. I hope so.

Daniel Ross

FUN

In Northfield, there is a park. The Clown Swing is not there anymore, but when it was, they sure had fun. It had two swings, and instead of going back and forth, it went in a circle. I used to get them swinging so fast on that thing. You'd grab a hold of one swing and go around in circles as fast as you could, then let go. The one you had a hold of would take off lickety-split. They would scream with delight the faster it would go.

When I used to clean two grain elevators next to each other, you didn't have to travel on the street to get there. I used to let them ride on the hood of my Delta 88, very slowly, of course. When I got the van – that ended. Then I let them ride in the back with the hatch open. It got to the point when Tia wanted to walk to the next grain elevator, so I let her. Sometimes she would race me over there. Though I tried, I could never beat her. I had to go around the railroad tracks, so I always lost.

At one grain elevator, there was a train driven by my friend, Gene. He would see us walking out to the tracks. He would slow way down and stop to allow the girls and I to get on. Sometimes we'd ride on the rail. Sometimes we'd ride in the cab. Sometimes the girls would ride on Gene's lap and blow the horn while he switched the rail cars around.

Sometimes we'd drive the camper to work. If we got hungry, there would be food to cook in the camper. If the girls got tired, there would be a bed for them to sleep in. We had a lot of fun with that old camper.

One of my part-time jobs was working security at an auto auction. We would drive the different cars when I made rounds. Once there was a golf cart there, and Tia had fun steering the cart while I worked the gas.

One time, Aren had to work the night shift while I was working the night shift at the auto auction. I had her bring the kids over at midnight when she went to work. They just slept in the car while I sat in the guard shack.

When they were both very small, I built them a playhouse out of old cardboard boxes. The upstairs was relatively clutter-free at the time, and it made a good playroom. Aren and I installed a toddler gate at the top of the stairs so Ana would not fall. I never worried about Tia around stairs or ladders. She was always so sure-footed on them, and she was absolutely fearless. One time I didn't latch the gate, and Tia, being the big sister she was, held the gate shut and screamed until I came up there to latch it so Ana wouldn't fall down the stairs. Good girl!

I worked a lot when the kids were growing up, so did Aren. After the part-time cleaning business closed, I had to go to work full time. I couldn't spend as much time with them as I would liked to have. So, to compensate for the time I wasn't able to spend with them, we had what we called "Girls Day." It was usually on a Saturday, and taking turns. The girls could do anything with us they wanted to do. Sometimes they would choose a movie. Other times Tia would choose fishing. Once during the flood of '97, they wanted to see the flood waters. Sometimes it would be skateboarding at a local park or riding bikes.

I would try to spend as much time as I could one-on-one with them. But when I would try to spend one on one time with Tia, Ana would stand at the door and look so dejected. When I'd see her, it was like a knife stabbing into my heart. It seemed, for some reason, when I'd try to spend time with Tia, something would go wrong. Once, I tried taking her fishing in the boat. We got out in the middle of the lake, and the motor stopped. It would NOT start again. We finally ended up being towed by another boater back to dock. On the way home, the boat trailer had a flat tire, so that's where I had to leave it. Once, we were going to make a couple dozen deviled eggs, Tia and me. When I got the eggs boiled, however, the shells wouldn't peel. Nothing like this ever seemed to happen with Ana and me. Fate, I guess.

For some reason, the kids would figure out electronics faster than I would. They figured out how to work my web cam, and they would make up these little skits to entertain themselves. My favorite was Bob and Bill, the reporters. Tia was Bob in the studio, and Ana was Bill on assignment. They would report on Trixie (pet dog) in the neighborhood. When Ana was finished, she would say, "back to you, Bob." They even figured out how to make a stop-motion film. Films about a car traveling on a table or a stuffed animal eating candy and peeing after it was done. I have a collection of these skits on the computer at home.

When they were little, and I was cleaning the local grocery store floors, I would put them on the auto-scrubber and let them ride while I cleaned the floors. I would also chase them with the buffer. I think they were scared of it at first, but as they got older, it got fun to be chased by the buffer.

When Tia was very young, she would ask me if she could do something. And if I said no, she would put her arms down, hunch over and walk sadly away. It got to the point when I would imitate her by putting my arms down and following her as she walked sadly away. After a while, it would turn into a chase. Instead of being sad, Tia would run from me, laughing.

When Tia was very little, I had her, and I do a play. I recorded it on audio cassette tape to send to Uncle Joe. It was from the movie, The Secret of Nihm. Tia played Mrs. Brisby, and I played the owl. Tia was a natural actress. I never sent that tape, and it should be in the house somewhere. After we were done, Tia asked me if she could watch a movie on tape. I told her no because I wanted to tape more for Uncle Joe. "Can I watch a movie, daddy?" She asked.

"No," I answered. "Why, why, why daddy?" When I didn't answer right away, she asked, "Because I'm a bad girl?" Talk about a knife going through your heart. "No, Tia, you're not a bad girl. You're a very good girl." I told her I loved her.

When I would push Ana on the swing, I would stop and stand in front of her. I would bend over and pretend to pick something up. She would laugh and kick me in the butt, and I would fall over. This would happen again and again until my butt got sore. And she loved it.

The Make Me Laugh Game consisted of me trying to make the girls laugh, and the girls could let me. "Starting now," I'd say. Sometimes, all I'd have to do was look at them. Then that wouldn't work anymore. Then I'd make a face. Or a funny sound like, "mee, mee, mee, mee, mee, mee." They would explode with laughter. This was a fun game.

The Movie Lines Game was played when I said a line from one of their movies, like, "Would you please come down to dinner." They would have to guess the movie. Or "That must be terribly uncomfortable. Can't you get down?" They would have to guess The Wizard of Oz. Later, the game morphed into the next line. For instance, I would say, "Would you please come down to dinner?" They would have to say, "I'm not hungry!" We had a lot of fun games.

Lie and Lie

When we were in bed, we would play the game lie. For instance, I'd be lying in bed, and I'd say, "I like going to work. Then Ana would be lying in bed, and she would say, "I like doing chores. Tia would be lying in bed, and she'd say, "I like doing the dishes. On and on it would go.

Joo Joo Flop

This was a card game. I made up sort of on the line of Gin. You had to discard a card before you either picked one from the deck or the pile. The first person to get three of a kind and two of a kind in their hand won. The kids were extremely good at this game.

Make Me Funny, Daddy

When Tia was two or three, she loved to be tickled. I would tickle her, and while she laughed, I'd say, "It's funny, isn't it funny?"

So, every time she wanted to be tickled, she'd say, "I want you to make me funny, daddy."

Tia and Ana Singing Me to Sleep

I think both of them did this. First, they would sing or hum, "Lullaby and good night." I would pretend to go to sleep, and they would rudely wake me up. I would act surprised and annoyed at being woke up. It would be repeated again and again and again. They got so excited doing this. I remember Tia would get so riled up doing it again and again.

Tia on Headphones

One of my earliest memories of Tia's appreciation for music came with her listening to a tape on my headphones. She would sing along with each song. She was so cute doing that. Her favorite tape was the blue tape. I can't even remember the name of the band. It was a religious band, as I recall. "There's a song that the children sing…" began one of the songs. I liked them too.

Mommy and Little One

One of the earliest games the kids would play was Mommy and Little One. I remember I would listen to them play, and their games were not unlike the games my brother and I would play. A lot of the times, Ana would play "The Director." She would say a line and then direct Tia to say something, "Now you say…" Ana would say.

Ditta Ditta Ditta

Though the girls only played this game once, for some reason, it sticks in my head. Probably because it was so funny. When they were in the back seat of the car, I heard them say, "Ditta, ditta, ditta." Then, "Dit, dit, dit, dit dit, dit, dit." So, when I got home, I asked Tia, "What does ditta, ditta, ditta mean?" She explained that they were deer walking across the street. Ana explained when a car passed us, the dit, dit, dit, dit, dit was the deer running from it. Tia told me that the aaaahhh was the deer getting hit by the car. Now, they didn't see me, but I retreated to my room and laughed, man. That was so funny to me. Even now, as I'm writing this, I'm laughing my ass off!

Buster

Buster was a stray dog dragging a chain. The kids played with it for, I think, a day and a half. Finally, I knew this dog belonged to somebody, so I called the police and asked them if anyone lost a dog dragging a chain. They told me, "Yes." And they'd be over to pick the dog up. My kids had so much fun with that dog they hated to give him back. When the cops came to get it, Tia and Ana appeared to have nothing to do when the dog was gone. I looked out the playroom window, and Tia was crying. "Oh no!" I ran out the door and headed straight for her. Tia saw me coming and put her arms up to receive me. As I held her, crying, I knew I had to get them a dog.

The Flying Suit

One time, while I was at work, Tia and Ana got the urge to fly. So, they dreamed up a plan. They would construct a flying suit. They made it out of black material. They cut the suit and sewed it together. They actually put a lot of work into it and a lot of effort. Tia talked Ana into taking the maiden voyage. She was to climb to the top of the camper and jump off. To make sure Ana didn't get hurt, Tia drug a mattress outside just in case the suit didn't work. Needless to say, Ana was a little apprehensive to jump off the camper. I think that's when I caught them.

"What are you doing up there, Ana?"

"We made a flying suit," explained Tia.

Who was I to tell them they couldn't fly? There was a mattress on the ground, So I let them try. Ana still didn't want to jump, so I suggested she come down the ladder halfway and jump. She did, but she didn't fly. "No, she's got to be up all the way," said Tia.

"Why? To get her air speed up?" I asked. Tia agreed. I had to put a stop to it because what if I was at work and they tried it with mama asleep. There wouldn't be anyone to take Ana to the hospital. So, I made them promise never to do it when I was at work.

The Fence at the Telephone Company

There was a tall, six-foot fence in back of the Telephone Company that the kids used to climb. I can't believe how fearless they were on ladders and fences. I remember Tia had a little apprehension climbing it with her sister. I didn't push her to do it. I told her she didn't have to. In the end, Tia mastered her fear and climbed it like a pro. I was never the kind of parent to say, "no, you can't climb that ladder or fence. I felt that by letting them master something like that would help their confidence and self-esteem.

The Ass Burn's Joke

I told the kids a joke when they were close to being teens. I knew it was probably over Ana's head but not Tia's. I heard the joke when I was in school. I was about twelve. It goes like this: A woman needed something to cure her headache, so she went to the store to buy some aspirin. While she was there, she bought a few more items. When she was on her way home, on the bus, she realized she'd left her aspirin on the counter at the store. She yelled out, "My ass burns, my ass burns!" The bus driver yelled back, "Well, hang it out the window!" Tia didn't get it at first, but I watched her face, and as if someone had switched on a light, her face lit up, and she started laughing.

Catching Light Bugs

I remember one of the things we did for entertainment, that was cheap when the kids were young, was to drive to a place in the country on Hwy 19 to catch fireflies. They called them light bugs.

Looking at Stars

Similar to catching light bugs was putting a mattress on top of the camper and driving to the same place on Hwy 19 to look at stars. What was really neat, I thought, were the falling stars and the Northern Lights. This was something we could do that didn't cost much money because we didn't have much money. I think the kids will remember it for the rest of their lives.

Steering the Car at the Grain Elevator

We had a lot of fun when I was working the business. Not all of it was fun, but we seemed to have fun between jobs. I would put the kids on my lap. One at a time, of course. I let them steer the car from one grain elevator to the next. Since it was in an empty parking lot in the middle of the night, there was no danger. I would work the break and gas pedal.

The Convenience Store

Also, between jobs, we used to take a snack break at the convenience store in Prior Lake. It's not there anymore, but we would always seem to be there when the cops were there. The kids got to know them by their names. We also met a very good friend of ours there by the name of Bill. Bill worked behind the counter and seemed to love it when the girls would come to visit. Bill also went to our church. He had all the patience in the world for Tia and Ana.

Chasing Tia

Tia always loved to be chased. When I would catch her, she would scream with delight. She used to get so excited when I chased her. I don't care how old you are, all girls like to be chased, and all girls like to be caught. Ana liked to be chased, too, but when I caught her, it seemed she thought the game was over. She'd get mad that I'd caught her. I'd tell her the game wasn't over when I caught her. It was just that she'd have to run away again.

I See, Yahh!

Once when I was chasing Tia, she must have been four or five. She ran into the playroom and hid under the baby crib. I knew she had run into one of the bedrooms, but I couldn't find her. I entered the playroom and said, "I see yahh!" But I didn't. I didn't know where she'd run. But she screamed and emerged from under the crib, and I caught her. But that was the only time that worked. She got wise to my tricks, and I could only fool her once.

Chasing Tia Around the Kitchen

Another time when I was chasing Tia, she ran into the kitchen. She would run around the kitchen and through the bedroom, and through the kitchen again. She had run into the kitchen, and I stopped in the dining room to wait for her. She came out of the kitchen looking back, expecting to see me chasing her from the other direction. She didn't even know I was waiting for her as she approached. When she turned and saw me right there waiting for her: her face lit up, and she screamed. I always thought she was so cute when her face would light up in excitement.

Chasing Tia to the Top Bunk

My thing with Tia was chasing her. I would chase her to the top of her bunk. She would flatten herself out against the wall just out of reach, and she knew there wasn't anything I could do to get her. Smarty pants!

Wrestling Ana

My thing with Ana was wrestling. She would jump on top of me to begin the wrestling match. I would try to hold her off, but I was extremely fat at the time, and this little girl was actually pretty strong. Ana would pin me to the mattress when she got older, and for a time, I couldn't figure out how she kept me pinned to the bed. I thought, "How can this little girl have super-human strength?" Finally, I was able to figure out her secret. She was holding onto the handles of the mattress. There was no way I could get up until she'd let me up. Then there were the tickling missiles and the tickling bomb. She liked being tickled when she was little, but when she got older, she would catch my hand in midair and deflect my tickling missile with pinpoint accuracy.

Other times when I'd wrestle Ana, she would accidentally bump my glasses off. They would be hanging there by one temple. She'd look at me and laugh, man!

Chasing with the Sword

When the kids were older, about eleven or twelve, I'd chase them with a dull-bladed sword that I had hanging on the wall. I would put on my Civil War Hat and yell, "Charge!" And the game was on. It got to the point that the neighborhood kids would get involved. I'd chase all of them. In fact, they would come to my house and request to be chased, "Can you chase us with the sword?"

Pulling Them Down the Hill

When the kids were little, one of the things we used to do that was inexpensive was to take them to a rest area that was wooded. It had a playground. My wife and I would let them play all day if they wanted to. We snapped some good photographs of the kids there. We still have them today. One of the things I used to do was pull them down the hill on a blanket. That was fun for them, and I think I had more fun watching them have fun.

McDonald's

Another place we used to take them was the playground at McDonald's. Especially in the winter, this was good for them because there were always kids there to play with. We'd let them play all day, and if they got hungry, McDonald's was the place.

"Stop Throwing Candy!"

One of my favorite things I did with the kids was to go to movies. We saw everything at the movies like Narnia, all three Lord of the Rings, The Emperor's New Groove. A fun thing to do in a theater is shoot M &M's. You can only do this in a crowded movie theater, though. That way, you have less of a chance to get caught. You wet your thumb and forefinger. Then place an M & M between them. Then apply pressure, and the M & M shoots a good two, three rows in front of you. You want to hold it down at your waste when you do it. That way, nobody sees. During one of the Lord of the Rings movies, we put up such a barrage that the people in front of us were getting annoyed. I shot one and hit a man in the back of the head. He turned around with an angry look on his face, probably expecting to see some mean boys, but all he saw was a middle-aged man and two sweet little girls. Finally, the usher came out and shouted, "All right! Stop throwing candy!" That was the end of it.

Sledding

Another thing they used to do for fun was sledding. When they were little, after a big snowstorm, I would have the driveway plowed. I would ask the snowplow driver to pile as much snow as he could in the front yard by the tree. He was always glad to do it. Then they would slide down the makeshift hill. Another place I'd take them to slide was a tall, long hill in Northfield. Even I slid down that. I'll never forget Ana's first time down that hill. I didn't know she'd start clear at the top, but she did. Both of them were fearless. I remember seeing out of the corner of my eye someone coming down the hill so fast. It was like a streeeeak. I heard Ana exclaim, "Holy Smokes!" As more and more kids would show up at the hill, it got more and more dangerous as kids would slide down the hill right into other kids, knocking them down. It seemed like Ana would always get hit. So, we would leave when the hill got crowded.

Boh, Boh, Boh

One of my earliest memories of playing with Tia as a baby was tickling her with my hair. She'd get so excited and kick those little legs. Another game was when Tia would be voiceturizing in her crib. I would put my hand on her mouth and lift it up again so it sounded like "Boh, Boh, Boh, Boh."

The Candy Dinner

Once, we had a dinner consisting of Brach's Candy, malted milk balls, and chocolate-covered nuts. Oh, and chocolate milk. We only did this one time, but I heard about it the rest of their lives. "Can we have a candy dinner?"

The Cheese Tasting Party

I once bought several different cheeses just to let the kids try some different foods. Ana's favorite was Gouda, and Tia's favorite was Gjetost, a kind of goat cheese.

THINGS THEY SAID
"Oh, My God!"

On Christmas, I would give them Christmas money. It was whatever I could afford, ten, fifteen, twenty dollars. Christmas of 2006, I had been working a lot of overtime, so I gave them each $50. I gave Ana a fifty-dollar bill in the office. She said thanks and walked away. She got to the dining room when she finally looked at what I had given her, and I heard, "Oh my God!" It was so cute. She wasn't expecting $50 from me. She immediately told Tia.

"Look At That Car"

I don't remember where we were coming home from, but Ana must have been 5 or 6 when we passed a car lot. She said, "Look at that car up there, presenting…" to Tia. When I looked, I saw a car that looked like it was up on a stage.

"Hi! I'm Ana!"

When Ana was just two, when she'd meet someone for the first time, she would say, "Hi! I'm Ana!" She was such a friendly little girl, even at two. This was just one of those Ana things.

"Look at That Mess"

When Tia was upset, she would cry. When she'd cry, I held her in my arms, usually face down on my shoulder. Once when she was done crying, she looked at the wet spot she had made on my shoulder and said, "Look at that mess." I told her it was okay and that was her shoulder to make any kind of a mess she wanted on.

"The Mosquito"

When Tia was just eight months old, we were out on the back porch. A mosquito landed on Tia's leg, and I squished it. Tia, who had a command of the English language early on, said, "Why?" It was barely discernable, but you could hear it was the question, "why." I couldn't believe she was talking at such a young age, but I answered her anyway. I said, "Because it would have hurt you."

"This Is The Life!"

One night, Ana had a severe asthma attack, so I took her to the hospital, where they admitted her. When I came back to see her the next day, she was sitting in bed. When she saw me, she said, "Dad, this is the life. Any time I'm hungry, they give me ice cream, and they have cable TV." I knew from that point on I didn't have to worry about her being homesick. I think she was about seven at the time.

"Pretty Little Dress"

When Tia was four, we bought her a long, pink dress. She loved that dress. She wore it all the time. She even wore it after she outgrew it. From that point on and most of her life, she loved "pretty little dresses."

"Shot Op!"

Teenagers always argue. When Ana would argue with Tia, she would say, "Shot op!" That was one of the things only Ana could say.

"Tia Woman"

When Tia was only three, she announced, "I'm Tia, Tia woman." Her mother and I just cracked up. I don't even know where she got that from.

"Daddy Dear and Mommy No"

Again, when Tia was only two, she called me Daddy Dear because that's what her mother referred to me as. When Tia would look throughout the house for mommy, I would set her down and try to tell her as simply as I could that mommy wasn't here by saying, "Mommy, No." The name stuck. Now she referred to her mother as "Mommy No."

"Tarakian"

Maybe it was a mistake on my part, but I let them watch the movie "Heavy Metal." In it, there was a woman warrior called a tarakian. Ana would run around the house in her swimming suit and, carrying a plastic sword, would say, "Look, daddy, I'm a tarakian bitch."

Tia's First Montage

"Hi" and things Tia said. Tia had command of the English language early in life. Her first word at three months old was "Hi." As she turned one and a half, she was already saying four-syllable words like "watermenon" and five-syllable words like

"Hippopotamus." Even when she'd mispronounced a word, it made sense like peeti was pizza. Later she would say things like, "I'm full to this," and "she's at sleep," or "young an adult." When she was very young, she would tell me, "Drive koo foo," which meant drive careful. I'll never forget when Tia would sing to the song, "Rocky Top Tennessee. It would come out, "Rocky Talk in a Sea'. Other things she would say, "I did that!" when something would fall over by itself or "down the drain in my mouth," were comical. "Mommy, Daddy' she would say enthusiastically at age one and a half. When I asked her what a pin was, she told me it was an owee pokee. An animal was a "butty butty." When her mother and I would take her to the park, she would see all the kids out there playing. She would leave the car and shout, "Hi! Kids!" To describe something that was tasty, Tia would call it, "So gosh good." I still use that saying today.

"What's My Pet Name?"

One time, when I told Tia I didn't want anyone else to call Ana "Na" because that was my pet name for her, Tia, always looking to put herself on an equal playing field with her sister, said, "Well, what's my pet name?" I told her, "Tia Girl." She said, "Oh, yeah!" That satisfied her. XXO

"I Won, I Won Too"

When Tia was playing with Polly, a friend of hers, she didn't know I was looking out the bathroom window at them. Polly said, "If I catch this," meaning the ball, "you can't win.' And she threw the ball up and caught it. She said, "I won!" Tia said, "I won too!" Polly looked at her rather perplexed, but it was Tia's way of always being positive. She seldom got mad. When she got older, into her teenage years, she got mad more. But she was the only young woman I've ever known who was absolutely beautiful when she was mad!

Tia's Second Montage
"This is Candy"

When Tia was three, I gave her a piece of toast with sugar on it. She took one bite, looked at it, and said, "This is candy." Another time, after coming home from the store, she opened a bottle of Vitamin C without me knowing it. I heard her say, "This is icky candy." When I used to play horsey with her on my back, she would say, "Getty on, daddy, getty on!" Which meant getty up.

Ana's First Montage

When Ana was twelve, approaching her teenage years, when she would talk on the telephone or text on the computer, one of her sayings was, "Okie dokie." She would say this when she was about to sign off or hang up the telephone. She said it as a closing to a conversation. It's a good thing the kids will never see the things I'm writing in this notebook. Some of them may embarrass them. But as a dad, they are memorable.

Even when Ana was little, and she would mispronounce words, at least they made sense. After a long day, she would start to stumble and fall. I knew it was time for bed. When she would fall down, she would look at me to see if I would send her to bed. She would exclaim, "I just stumbode!"

Another thing she would say when she was tiny was "eggy eggy eggy." I'm not quite sure what it meant, but maybe that was her name for an egg. Ana would always tell me she loved me. She would say," I love you, dad." I would say," I love you too, Ana." So, it got to the point that she would say, I love you too, Dad.", first. She was so sweet. XXO When I bought Tia her first hamster, I thought Ana was a little too young for one. So, I bought her a cat toy (a mouse). It had pretend fur on it, and it looked quite real. Ana took it with joy. Halfway home, she said, "Dad, it can't move!" Sweety, she must have thought it was real. I think she was two at the time.

At a young age, we discovered Ana had asthma along with me. So, I had all the stuff already, asthma inhaler and Nebulizer. Ana would wake me up in the middle of the night and say, "Dad, I'm sick, I'm sick!" That meant she was having an asthma attack, and she needed to go on the Nebulizer. Another example of Ana saying things that weren't in the dictionary but made sense was: I turned down the wrong street. One of them asked me where I was going. I said I think I was lost. Ana said, "Well, don't keep going this way, dad. You're just going to get loster." It made absolutely perfect sense. I turned around and went back. One of the things that really cracked me up that Ana said was when we were in bed and the lights were off. She claimed that she could really act out dying. I told her I could too, and I made the sound of me dying. "No, you can't, dad," Ana said in perfect pitch, black darkness. "Your tongue's probably hangin' out." I just lost it laughing because it was hanging out.

Ana never liked spiders. She would call Tia to kill spiders for her. One day I started singing a song by Jim Stafford to her, "I don't like spiders and snakes." She promptly told me she didn't mind snakes which was true. She caught them all the time. Both girls did.

"Crunch Him?"

When Ana was very young, the word "chew" was "crunch." We were watching a nature program where a lion was chasing a gazelle. I told her that lion wants to crunch that little thing. She looked at me with utter disbelief and said, "Crunch him?"

"'Mon 'Sco"

When Ana was two, she would tell Tia, "' Mon, 'Sco!" This meant, "Come On! Let's Go!"

"Oat-O-Meal"

This was one of Tia's words to describe oatmeal.

"Humpy Dumpy"

Humpty Dumpty was humpy dumpy.

Things I Did to Show My Love for Them
Sad Girls

When the girls were sad or mad or hurt, I would put them on my lap. Wrapping my arms around them, I'd say, "It's okay, I'm here. I've got you now, trying to comfort them.

Chinese Fighting Fish

Ana had a Chinese Fighting Fish. She loved that fish. She'd spend time with it every day. One morning I found it dead in the fishbowl. Knowing that she would be crushed, I hurried to the pet store to buy another one before she woke up. When she woke up, she headed immediately downstairs to spend time with her fish. I heard her say, "Hey, he's got a little red on his tail now! Maybe he's growing up." I don't think she ever found out.

Following the Kids to Moldy's

When Tia was four, I let her walk to Moldy's Gas Station by herself to get some candy. I followed her all the way down to make sure she was okay. When I saw her come out, I hurried back home so she would think she walked there totally on her own. When Ana was four, I did the same with her. I don't think they ever found out they had a guardian looking after them.

Standing Behind Them

When they would do something for the first time, it was scary. So, I stood behind them, with my arms around them for support. When they turned on the washing machine or turned on the water for the first time, It's very scary. It's very scary to turn on the water in the sink. I remember my first time. It was at a Podiatrist's Doctor's office. You don't know which way to turn it off.

Ana's Favorite Shirt

Ana had a shirt that she was very fond of. It was pink with little ruffles on it. Like Tia, she loved clothes. One day she spilled meat sauce on it. Oh, My God! You'd think the world had come to an end. She thought her favorite shirt was ruined. I took the shirt to wash it. I didn't trust the washing machine because if the stain didn't come out, I wouldn't know about it. So, I washed the shirt by hand in the sink with an old washboard. I got the stain out and showed it to Ana. "Thanks, Dad!" she exclaimed. This happened one other time, and again I washed it by hand. Aren thought it was the greatest thing in the world to do.

Cried With Them

Unknown to the girls, when I held them when they cried, I cried with them. I wonder if I'm the only father to do that. Sometimes I think I was born with the emotions of a woman.

Sick

One of my jobs I thought was extremely important was taking care of my kids when they were sick. This let them know that they were very important. My kids were fiercely independent. But when they were sick, they turned into little kids again. I would fuss over them, taking their temperature and making sure they were warm. I wonder if they remember that?

Drawings

One of their hobbies was drawing. They were good. My favorite that Tia drew were wolves in Native American garb: like bows and arrows. My favorite that Ana would draw were the loots, a fictitious animal that resembled an Egyptian Jackle. Their drawings were so good. I didn't want them to get ruined. So, I put each one that I found in a document protector and put them all in a three-ring binder. There must have been a hundred of them. I wonder how good their drawings are now.

Listened

Before the kids came, I heard that it was important to listen to your kids. I firmly believed in that. When they were little, and they were just busting with news about a new bug they had found or something they did or achieved, I would always listen to them. No matter what I was doing, whatever they had to say took precedence. I think this added to how close the girls and I were when they were little.

Red Face

Sometimes when the kids were upset, it was hard for me to tell. With Ana, it was simple. Her nose would get red. A red dot would appear under her right eye. That's how I knew she was upset. Tia, on the other hand, would make no secret of her feelings, running away crying and laying on her bed face down. I would go into her room and take her from behind and say, "Tia, oh Tia. Honey, ohhhh!" I held her until she felt better.

THINGS THEY DID THAT WERE MEMORABLE
Rattle Snake

When Tia was about ten, we were at work cleaning the big grain elevator. I sent her out to the van to get something. She came back to tell me there was a noise like a rattlesnake in the van. Though a rattlesnake in Minnesota would be unlikely, it was not unheard of. I went out to the van, and as soon as I opened the door, there it was, the sound of a rattle. Great! I didn't have anything to kill it with. It turned out to be a can of WD-40. Something was on the spray knob with just enough pressure to make it sound like a rattle.

Climbing Up in Laps

When Ana was barely able to walk, she would climb up in peoples laps that she liked. Once there was a young boy at a doctor's office whose lap she climbed up in. She couldn't even talk yet.

Stage

One of my fondest memories were the kids up in front at the movie theater pretending like they were up on stage. Tia would hide behind the curtain, and Ana would say, "Presenting Mrs. Tia!"

Tia in the Hospital

When Tia was just five days old, she got jaundice. She had to be taken back to the hospital. They put her in an incubator for a couple of days. Tia had motor control very early. When the nurses put eye patches over her eyes to protect her eyes from the ultraviolet lights, Tia moved the patches off her eyes. This was much to the disbelief of the nurses and her parents.

Picture Frame

One of the cutest things Ana used to do was to hold a Styrofoam frame up to her face and peek through. It looked just like a picture frame.

On the Dock

One time when we were cleaning the big grain elevator, Tia found a lawn chair in the dumpster. I didn't want her to keep it because it had a hole in it. But she wanted it. So, I told her if she could sit in the chair while I drive the van away, she could keep it. I was thinking that she wouldn't do it. When she told me she would, I couldn't go back on my word, so I left her sitting on the dock. I think I was more scared than she was. I was almost in a panic when I drove as fast as I could, crossed the railroad tracks, turned around, and came back. Well, she earned her chair. Brave little sh**!

Ana Eating Corn

I used to watch my kids when they did stuff like play or read. One time I was watching Ana eat an ear of corn. She was so cute. I think the corn was bigger than her face. Halfway through eating, she asked, "Ossum corn, Tia? She was two.

Tia Eating an Apple

I started taking the kids to work with me early on. I took Tia to the big grain elevator when she was three days old. One day I had Tia with me at the greenhouse because it was cheaper than hiring a babysitter. I wanted her with me. I let her run around while I cleaned. I was dusting when I heard, "gulp, gulp, gulp." When I turned around to see what she was into, she was sitting on the floor eating a green apple. I didn't even know she was into solid foods. She's liked green apples ever since.

The Rest on the Floor

When Ana was a baby in the highchair, she would eat a little food, and the rest would be slung on the floor. When this was done, we knew she was full.

Tia Flapping Her Wings

When Tia was a baby in the highchair, Aren would be getting her food ready. Tia would be impatient, would flap her arms in frustration because the food wasn't coming fast enough.

Belly Button

Another memorable thing Ana did as a baby was trying to stick her finger in my belly button. I only let her do it once because, as a baby, she had sharp fingernails. It hurt!

Tia Dancing

I have Three examples of Tia dancing. The first was when she was a baby. Before she could talk, she was on my dad's lap, trying to get up and dance with cousin Alyssa. Second, when she was barely able to walk, she would dance to my music. She would stand right up and dance. Where did she get this from? Mom and I weren't dancers. Thirdly, as a toddler, she danced all night at Uncle Jake's wedding. She'd take a break to help herself to some cake and back to dancing.

Ana Backing Away from Olag

When Ana would play Draken, after buying weapons from Olag, she would back away from him so as not to let Olag see the character Rynn's butt. It's just something that stuck with me.

The Dragonfly

Once when I was cleaning for the part-time business, I had Tia along with me. I let her play while I cleaned. When I got done cleaning the restroom, I came out and heard her talking. She was saying, "eye, eye, eye." When I went to investigate, she was in the lunchroom with a dead dragonfly on the table. It looked huge next to her. She was so inquisitive; she didn't care if she was holding a great big bug. I would never have done that at her age. Even today, I'm a little squeamish about big bugs.

Dancing with Uncle Joe

While visiting my dad in Florida, my brother Joe was there. He picked up Ana and danced with her. Later, Tia said to me, "Why didn't he dance with me? I'm the one who knows how to dance!" Later we were at a nightclub, and I pulled Joe aside and told him Tia was a little depressed because she didn't get to dance with him, so, after dinner, when the music was playing, Joe asked Tia to dance. She was so excited she jumped up and said, "Yeah, yeah!" While I was finishing my dinner, I heard the people say, "Aaahhh." When I looked up, Tia was dancing with Joe. Her arm was around him, and her cheek was against his stomach as she was dancing a slow dance. It was so cute!

Ana Playing the Piano

Ana never took piano lessons. But every time she sat down at a piano, her plunking sounded musical. Not just the random noise plunking a child would make. It actually sounded musical. She would make up these musical compositions that actually sounded good. I think that it was a mistake on my part not to have gotten her into some lessons. Number one, we couldn't afford them. But she may have been the next prodigy.

Lessons on Tape

From the time my kids were able to crawl, I taught them. One of my favorite things was to place lessons on tape for them to do. For instance, when I was teaching them the sounds of the vowels, I'd say, "What two sounds does an "a" make?" They would respond "a and ah." Then I'd say, "Okay, but I'm gonna fool you now. What two sounds does an "o" make?" They would respond, "oh and ah." I would praise them on the tape. Later, their spelling tests were on tape. Their spelling reviews were fun. I would record on tape, "spell the word, those." They would respond, t-h-o-s-e. Then I'd record something like, "Okay, now here's a hard word, spell, there." Then they would respond. It got to the point that they would talk to the recorder. I would watch them through the door. It was so cute.

Things They Did to Show Their Love for Me

Both would mix up my soda water when I had heartburn. Both would wash my clothes because I was too fat to climb up the stairs. Tia would cook macaroni and cheese for me. Ana would make grilled cheese sandwiches for me using the toaster. Once when I had an infection between my toes, they would very carefully doctor it. Both would take care of me when I was sick. Ana would always pop the boil on my chest. When they made popsickles, they always saved the last one for me. XXOO

MISCELLANEOUS MEMORIES
I Left the Kids at the Gas Station

I'll never forget the time I left the kids at the gas station. I was upset that I couldn't find wiper blades to fit my old Delta '88. I drove all the way to the big grain elevator. I turned around to tell them how quiet they were and . . .no kids. I drove back at break-neck speed, almost in a panic. I pulled into the gas station, and there they were. "Why did you forget us?" asked Tia. "I was upset about something," I answered. Tia told me the man at the gas station said, "Did he forget ya? He'll be back."

The Blue Horses

Some kids have security blankets. Ana had two blue horses she would carry constantly. She would try to pick something up, and I would tell her, "You can't pick that up with a handful of horses." She loved horses.

Ride to Live, Live to Ride

I didn't want the art of riding horses to die with their generation. I thought I would have to teach them to ride horses. Nope, they acted like they were born in a saddle. They were absolutely fearless of them.

Bedtime Stories

I would always make up stories to tell them. One of their favorite characters was Gwendelin. Gwendelin was a very naughty little girl. There were hundreds of Gwendelin stories. They would always start off like this: Once upon a time, there was a little girl named Gwendelin and Gwendelin was walking home from school one day…and on it would go. Gwendelin would do disobedient, naughty, almost wicked things. After about 200 Gwendelin stories, she bought a pumpkin, carved a face in it, and began to worship the devil. And she became 'The Dark Lord of the Seth. (which scared Jeremy). From then on, her stories became sinister. Until one night, an old man was crossing the street, and Gwendelin was going to mess with him. The old man turned to face Gwendelin and raised a cross. From then on, an epic battle took place. Each using their power against one another. When it was over, Gwendelin lay down in the street, her demons gone. From then on, she was a good little girl. It was Tia that pointed out, Gwendelin became boring after that. From time to time, I'd let the kids exercise their own imagination. Most of them weren't bad. Ana's stories, however, would begin like this: Once upon a time there was a little horsey…

Ana, Three Days Old

The next story I have to tell isn't very funny. In fact, it makes me cry. But I think it needs to be told for posterity. When Ana was Three days old, we brought her home from the hospital. We had been up for such a long time we should have gone home and went to bed. Instead, we went to visit a co-worker and his wife. While we were there, Ana began choking. She couldn't breathe. Aren and I were in a panic. Aren told me to go out to the car to get the blue baby nasal aspirator. I said, "Aren, the aspirator won't work if she's choking! She replied, "We've got to try something!" So, I went out to get the nasal aspirator. While I was looking for it, I was thinking. Other people lose babies. I don't want to be one of them! I found the aspirator and rushed it back into Aren. She tried it and shouted, "It's not working!" Then she shoved the baby in my arms while she called 9-1-1. It's a good thing she did because I wasn't thinking straight. As I looked into that sweet baby's face, she closed her eyes. I thought she was dead. Then Aren shouted from the next room, "They say give her some shallow breaths!" Without thinking, I gave her four quick breaths and looked at her,…nothing!" I gave her four more. She opened her eyes and cried. Thank you, Father (God), I thought. The sound of her crying was the most beautiful sound in the world. Looking back on the experience, I think I was giving her the breaths too quickly–not letting her lungs exhale fully. That's why it took eight breaths. I had never done that before.

Tia Learning How to Ride a Bike

Tia, when she couldn't do something, she got so frustrated. This was the case when she was trying to learn how to ride a bike. I took her training wheels off and took her across the street to the park to practice. Each time she fell, she got more frustrated. She'd scream, "I can't do it!" I'd tell her, "You got to keep practicing. You'll get it!" But at the time, it seemed insurmountable to her. After several times of failure and tears, I let her go down to the park by herself because I wasn't sure if I was making her frustration worse. That, if she failed when no one was looking, it might be easier for her. I'll never forget, after several times of trying by herself, she came back to the house gleeful, "I did it, dad, I rode my bike!"I knew you could do it, Tia!" I said, and I hugged her. Soon she was riding like a pro. Later on, as she got older, she was riding over to her friend Suzie's place. I was a little apprehensive letting her travel so far and through the country, but she made it. She called me at work to ask me if she could go. I told her to take plenty of water (it was a hot day) and rest when you need to.

She's a Snot

Once when we came out from shopping at More 4, I was eating something in the van. I looked over at the car next to us, and there was a little girl imitating me eat. Only, she was mocking me very repulsively. I glanced back and saw Ana looking at her, and I said, "She's a snot." And Ana said, "I know."

You're Me

When I'd try to get the kids to do something they were scared to do, I'd tell them. I wouldn't tell you to do anything that would hurt you. Would I hurt me?" I wouldn't either. I was very protective of my kids. Maybe too protective. But kids are supposed to bury their parents, not vice-versa. I think it must be the most terrible thing in the world to bury your child.

The Red T-Shirt

I used to make my kids laugh. That was one of my jobs, I think. Once I shot my insulin in my stomach. I had a bright red T-shirt on, and after I shot myself, I said, "Oh no, I got some blood on my t-shirt. Ana laughed apparently because my shirt was red. I'm glad my kids had a sense of humor.

Tia's Baby Picture

When Aren and I took Tia to get her baby pictures, Aren took her in while I went to look at something. When I was done, I went back to the photographer. Tia saw me and started smiling and reacting at the sight of me. According to the photographer, they were having trouble getting Tia to smile for the camera. But as soon as I walked in, her face lit up. Tia and I were inseparable the first Three years of her life. We were the best of friends.

Ana Standing Up Against Halloween

I was never prouder of Ana when her Royal Ranger's teacher came out to tell me that Ana refused to participate in any Halloween activities. She said it was stupid and asked me why we were afraid of Halloween. I asked, "Is Halloween in 'your' Bible? If not, quit trying to put it in mine. These were people that professed to be Christian, and they were wondering why we didn't celebrate Halloween.

Tia Still Wanting to Suckle

When Ana came along, Tia had to give up suckling from mom. Mom would say, "You can have some cow's milk. But that wasn't good enough for Tia. One day when Ana was suckling, Tia wanted mom to hug her. I remember Tia complaining, but mom was busy with Ana. I remember holding my arms outstretched, inviting Tia to be hugged by me to let mom do her thing. Tia saw me and immediately climbed down off mom, ran, and jumped into my arms. This is just one of those things a dad would remember.

Dead Monarch Butterfly

When Tia was Two, there was a dead Monarch Butterfly on the sidewalk in front of the county market. I wanted Tia to see it, but she refused. She was scared of it. So, I bent down on one knee in front of it. I said, "See, it won't hurt you!" She crept up behind me and peered over my shoulder to look at it. She didn't like the butterfly, but she didn't mind a huge dragonfly.

Downstairs

I'd smoke in the basement. I'd bring my water glass down with me. Then, I'd go to bed and reach for my water and realized I'd left it downstairs. I'd send Tia down to get it, and she would until she started watching scary movies on TV. Then she wouldn't. So, I'd send Ana downstairs. Another time I sent Tia out to the van to get my water. When she was coming back in, I said, "Pumpkinhead." She ran up the stairs into the house and complained, "Dad! That was a real scary movie!" "Well, why watch them then!" I replied.

Bat Catching Business

Tia and Ana put up flyers offering to catch peoples bats for them and remove them. I had no problem with it. I knew they could catch them without any problems. I'd see them flying around. I don't know if they got any takers. They would have been good at it.

Goose Pimples

When I wrestled the girls, I'd hug them and kiss them at the same time. I noticed when I'd kiss the girls on the left side of their necks. Goose pimples would rise on their right leg and vice-versa.

The Key-Hoo (pet kitty) Incident

We had to pick up cat food at a pet shop in Northfield. They were having an open house for a local animal shelter. We looked at all the animals. That was a mistake. We found this little Calico kitten. She was so cute; she would rub against my beard. We all fell in love with her. We decided to adopt her. But when they wanted over a hundred dollars for her, I decided no, no way, cats are free. All you need to do is open the paper. We went home. Ana cried all the way home. She opened a fortune cookie when she got home, and it said, "You will meet a lifelong friend." Ana lost all manner of composure. She started crying again. I saw her, and it was as though I was being stabbed in my heart. Then mom said she'd pay for her. We rushed back to the pet store to adopt her. I'm glad we were able to. I remember another time at the feed store. There was a box of chicks. The kids had so much fun playing with them and holding them. Mom and I did too. When it was time to leave, Ana said, Mom, can I have a chicky? Their little wings are so cute!" Of course, we didn't have any place to put a pet chicken. I felt so inadequate. I've wanted to have a farm all my life, but I never knew how to make my dream come true.

TALES OF THE PARANORMAL
Weasel
Our house is haunted. It's been very active over the years. I think the kids just accepted that fact. One time when Tia was awake, she saw, what looked like a weasel, come out of the wall, walk across the room in the air, stop at the foot of her bed, looked at her with red, glowing eyes, and ran into the wall.

Midnight Jumping
Before we had dogs, we just had a cat, Midnight. He would be laying on the floor, watching something as it were moving from one side of the room to the other. Then his head would stop, and he'd jump up and run to the other room. Whatever he saw or was seeing had scared him.

Something Walking Across My Bed
We got used to the water turning on, running for a while, then

turning off. Or the doors opening by themselves, the voices talking, then they stop when you listen to them. Several times I'd be in bed, and it felt like something jumped up in my bed and walked across it. Well, with three cats, I thought it was Midnight or Key-hoo. But when I looked for it, nothing was there. This happened about four or five times.

Three Foot Thing

Ana woke up in the middle of the night and saw a dark figure standing at the foot of her bed. It was about three feet tall. It was looking at her. She jumped under the covers. When she peeked out again, it was gone. Strangely, that night she was in the hospital with a severe asthma attack. I wonder if the two were connected.

Shadows on the Wall

The night Ana was in the hospital, Tia and I were home alone. After we'd gone to bed, Tia kept seeing shadows on the wall behind my bed. "Dad, there was a shadow behind your bed." I'd turn and look, and it would be gone. The next time it happened, I looked back and missed it again. Then Tia said, "Dad, this time there was a huge shadow behind your bed." What I should have done was get in Ana's bed and wait to see one. Instead, I got up and turned on the little light. With the light on, there were no more shadows. This satisfied Tia. "Thanks, Dad," she said. The shadow's must have been scaring her.

MEMORIES OF AREN
Midnight Rainbow

While driving home from work in the rain, I noticed in the East there was a moon, a full moon too. I looked to the West to see if there was a rainbow, and there was. I stopped the van at Highway 19. I can't remember the name of the other street. It was a small park and ride parking lot. I watched it for a little while. Then jumped in my van and ran home as fast as I could to get Aren because a rainbow in the dark was very rare. I woke her up and drove back to that spot to show her. It was about midnight when we got there. I had lived forty-two years and never saw a rainbow in the dark.

Editors note: These letters have been reproduced exactly as written. Spelling and grammatical errors included.

CHAPTER 17
My Faith, Past & Present

I have my personal views on God, His creation, and some of what the Holy Bible says. In one incident, I talked with someone of another faith and was surprised to learn that they felt sorry for me and that I grew up with the faith I had. It made me think about that! Do we all have our own perception of God? That is for those of us who believe God exists. I think that God is quite mysterious. I can't claim that I have seen God physically, but I believe I have seen Him in the spirit's actions in many different people. I believe I saw Him when I was severely ill with a very high fever when I was a child. I remember floating up toward the ceiling, and there was a very brilliant bright light. There was no voice, yet there was communication. I was expressing eager feelings to get back to myself in bed. I came down and kissed my own lips and was back to this life.

I grew up praying "The Lord's Prayer" in church and "Now I Lay Me Down to Sleep" at bedtime, and other prayers my mom made up.

At age 12, I was sitting in the living room thinking about God and praying for Him never to leave me. This, according to the Bible, is what God promises anyway. I am seeing that He doesn't leave me. I have felt alone many times, but that is just the way I have felt, and it's alright to admit how I truly feel.

I grew up learning about Jesus. He included everyone. He wanted everyone to live forever with Him. He was merciful to those that others looked down on. His unconditional love was unmatched by any other being that ever existed on this earth. I don't believe there will ever be anyone as brilliant as He was. He was great at reading thoughts. No one was ever able to outsmart Him in any situation. I need to keep returning to His wise words and find others on this planet that pray to Him for direction in their lives. Jesus is loving and brings us eternal joy when we know Him. He is the peaceful King of Kings forever. He is patient with sinners like Dan and me. His kindness extends to everyone that will understand that he is our best example. The fruits of the Holy Spirit: are love, joy, peace, patience, gentleness, goodness, faithfulness, meekness, and self-control. Jesus lived all these awesome characteristics. He also put cocky people in their place when they were wrong and where they belonged.

I believe that those who say there could not be a God are really saying that they know everything. When you think about that, is that really true? I believe that I know that I know a very tiny little bit about everything that there is to know. Knowledge about things yet to be discovered will be coming in the future! When you think about how "fearfully and wonderfully we were formed inside our mother's womb," that speaks volumes! One day, I believe that science will prove how many generations have come before us. Are we really evolved from fish or apes? Well, maybe if we eat them, maybe we are them! The old saying is that "food becomes YOU!" Haha! Thinking about how even our thoughts and dreams happen to me is way out of this world! Everything is too complex to leave out the possibility that there is an Almighty God that can do any possible thing! Think about that! There is far too much that is unexplainable to many humans.

Even the smartest people can't explain everything! There is so much more knowledge yet to be discovered than what our tiny minds can explain! God will reveal more and more about His creation and eventually more about His omniscience and omnipresence. We shall see!

Another thing I have learned is that our bodies seem to know how to work out the details, like the complicated process of changing food into more muscle or how it renews itself. For a few people, their bodies are smarter than their brains! It amazes me that someday we will know more! There must be more! There has to be a Creator of all these intricate details within us and outside of us into infinity! I like to think about infinity. It's endless! God is infinity. God is glorious and amazing! God has all the good answers to any question that we have.

I've had some WOW! Moments where it has struck me that there are extraordinarily sensitive people and critters around me. Dogs have noses that smell so many details and help solve health issues and crimes. Dogs also hear sounds that we humans don't hear. Eagles and hawks have the super acute vision to see a small mouse from way, far away. Bats sense their location with their built-in radars. All kinds of creatures have some special thing that's better than another. There are amazing people out there who never forget what they ate for breakfast ten and three-quarters years ago! I am in awe of people with photographic memories. I have been privileged to meet a young lady that remembers everything I ever said, like when I told her my daughters' birthday and the name of a couple of our cats. Many amazing people make the world a better and more interesting place. There are people whose brains calculate big math problems with no need for a calculator. If you think that is great, there's something even greater! It's what I believe. I believe that

God is what is infinitely greater than many of the amazing people here on Earth. God gives me hope for the future. I want something to look forward to. I will accept the amazing gifts that Almighty God has promised me. I want them for you too!

I found some old prayers that I wrote in a notebook when my girls were tiny:

> February 1995
> Dear God,
>
> Help me make a career decision! Help me know myself and to figure out where I would be most effective and enthusiastic with the abilities you have given me. I enjoy passing along information. I enjoy sharing information. I enjoy informing others about things there is to know. I love geography. I love art. I love art history. I enjoy learning about other cultures, past and present. Would I make a good college art/ Art History or Geography teacher? May your name be blessed. Amen!

> Dear God!
>
> You know our troubles long before we know about them. You know the answers to our problems long before we can figure out how we're going to solve them. Help us pay our taxes. Help us come up with the money to pay our taxes. Help me unconditionally love my husband and children. I need lots of help. Please channel your love through me to them. I need help from you so badly, so much! Help me not be so hard on myself and so irritable when things go wrong! Help my helplessness and my unbelief in what

you are able to do in this situation. Please help me handle things in this life YOUR WAY! Help me see! Help me love myself and my family, and others around me! I seem to fail to love unconditionally every time, or at least more than I do. Break me of this bad thing! The sooner, the better! May Your Name be praised, Almighty God.

————————

3-20-95

Help me, God! I'm in tears. I feel so inferior, helpless, fearful, worried, stressed out, and hated. I read what you said about worry in Matthew 6:25. I'm not doing too well, and yes, I seem to have the least amount of faith. Without you, God, I am nothing. I'd like to ask for boldness to face the day and not alone and, please, not with tears for others to see. Where my faith isn't, please make it 100% faith. I am discouraged, depressed, ashamed, and oppressed. It does not feel good. I feel motivated to be in a place where I'd be most productive. I really need to be cheered up. I really need to be bold. I really need to be 100 % filled with faith. I need peace and solitude. I need to be uplifted. I need to be able to speak and express myself. Please let Yourself, Almighty God, speak through me today. Teach through me this week. Allow me to let You lay out what you want to accomplish. Impart to me Your wisdom today and every day.

————————

Dear God,

I am very sad. Here on earth, sometimes I feel so alone. Financially I am alone. I am alone to buy groceries and take care of the house payment, gas bill, the electric bill, car gas bill, equipment loan, school loan, car repair bill, and property tax bill. I am alone as far as people go. Dan is gone as far as helping me with bills. $400 is all I asked for each month. He isn't able to pay. He uses the phone irresponsibly. I can stand it better knowing I have you, dear God. I am still in pain. Why do I have to be alone to manage everything? I feel I'm being taken advantage of. He bounces checks. He buys fast food. Now he's buying a van. Why? Do we need a van? Remind me somehow that You care very much for me. Touch me. You'll never leave me alone.

———————

Dear God,

The problem at work is my concern. I want to give the whole thing to you to take care of. Empower our 3-person team to get out to the customer some very good boxes. Give Godly wisdom to the supervisors to take good care of the matter and give the wisdom of handling the customer-to-customer service or whoever speaks directly to the customer. Give wisdom, patience, and understanding to them. Empower our team to produce boxes that please you and the customer. May those in power see and solve the problems and make them right. Forgive me of my foolish pride. Provide protection and security for my family and me. May Your will be done as you see the best fit. Give Your blessings to our company. Amen.

———————

October 1995
Dear God,

Please make me see clearly what is best career-wise. I have dreams of being a freshman-level art teacher in a college. I'm looking for a more fun career to get into. I enjoy playing by making something, yet I need a secure job. If it is to happen – it will fall into place. I really, really wish that I could make a career where I can include my family- my children, who need me to be their mother. I'm Yours, Almighty God. Whatever I do, turn it out for Your purpose. May Your Name be blessed! Amen.

I came back to this notebook. I read through my prayers. I started another prayer:

Dear God,

Here I am 21 years later, realizing again it's YOU I need and not any guy out there! Instead of texting a guy all evening and night, I should have talked to YOU! I still struggle with some lonely feelings, and I'm without a Significant Other. Almighty God, will YOU be the Significant Other I long for? Please hold me. Please enlighten me! Please help me meet others who give recognition to YOU!

I have been gainfully employed in a "day job"; however, getting into the groove where I can use my God-given talents has been like getting stuck in a maze. It seems that I've been unable to get through to my goals! I feel I have let God, my family, and myself down.

Finding a Significant Other has been difficult, and I've been much more accepting that there could be someone. I will not work hard at finding love as I did after my divorce. If they want me and we have a lot in common, they can do most of the work! God loves me for sure!

As I write, it is nearly Easter soon. One early morning when I was half awake with my eyes closed. I saw a thumbnail Etch A Sketch image silhouette of Jesus in my right eye. My mind recognized the image. I hadn't been thinking about the One that had saved my soul. It just appeared to me! Then, I saw an equally flared, four-pointed Etch A Sketch cross a moment later. Could someone please explain this phenomenon that came about with no effort? Our minds are more complicated than we can comprehend! Almighty God has a mind way far above our capabilities. Our Creator is exponentially more complex if we think we are unique and complex! Our absolutely amazing King of Kings will rule over all with His much-needed kindness and unconditional love.

I'm going to add my opinion that Almighty God accepts a microscopic speck-sized faith in Him to be included in the perfect future that will arrive one day. Only God knows when!

CHAPTER 18
Blessed With a Grandchild

My beautiful grandson arrived nearly nine years ago. Trees started to form buds, and birds began to return to sing their songs. He is our small family's blessing! He has a special place in this world. His mommy chose the gift of life for him. His birth father wanted the opposite of life when he was coming along. He did not know who was coming along, and it didn't matter to him at the time. He also didn't have enough respect for Tia. She was vulnerable to abuse. I am grateful he is here because he is my only grandchild and probably will be my only grandchild. His mesmerizing dark brown eyes resemble his auntie's, and his silky hair matches hers exactly. He's very tall next to his peers, with exceptional hand-eye coordination. As a young toddler, he used to balance objects on his crib bars, which impressed his grandma, mommy, and other family members. He once flicked his fingers toward a toy car into a coffee cup, successfully tipping it over. We enjoy watching him grow up. He sometimes worries about the future and the day ahead, whether it will turn out good or what. However, it seems for his sake that it turns out quite good, if not great. Worry seems to run in our family. Yes, we are told in the Bible not to worry about things, but some of our family members need extra encouragement for that problem!

Before we lived together, I would come over occasionally for a visit. This little boy's beautiful smile warmed me every time we got together. He is soft-spoken and calm, very thoughtful and careful. My precious grandson loves the Zucchini Chocolate Chip Cookies I bake for him, and he'll eat one right after another! Grandma happily sneaks a healthy vegetable into this delectable treat.

He works hard in school. His teacher says he's a leader that other children notice and often follow. He loves to work on puzzles and demonstrates excellent patience in challenging ones. Grandma has a lot of influencing to do. I need to give him gentle advice on what makes life better. I will advise him to work doing something he loves doing. I will talk to him about life after this life. I'll warn him about all the addiction traps I know. He will get good advice on keeping physical, spiritual, and financial health.

Grandson goes along with Grandma on nature walks while we talk about the many creatures and plants along the way. He is very diligent in his education and spells very well. He reminds Grandma to "do the God thing" by thanking God for grandsons, family, friends, and the gift of eternal life.

My grandson and I talk about spiritual matters. "Mommy doesn't believe God exists, but I do." "Mommy was hurt when she was little," I explained. We talk about whatever is on his mind, and before sleeping, we pray together.

Grandma is not particularly impressed with the digestive gases he brings into the conversation here and there, and Grandma lets him know in a "Minnesota Nice" way. I hope to involve him in beginning music lessons on the keyboard and the native flutes on which I play hymns and other music. We will play some percussion instruments like rain sticks, the Eagle Whistle, and the wooden frog.

We explore numerous playgrounds and make time for an occasional touch tag or ball tag game. He enjoys having Grandma try to catch him as we run, laugh, and play, enjoying good times in the fresh air and sunshine. My grandson appears to be primarily easygoing and shares fun activities with new friends while we are there.

Tia, my grandson, and I will continue to live together. We rely on each other for family support. I tried to include my younger daughter Ana in our goals. But she has her independent plans. I love seeing my offspring happy, as all loving parents and grandparents do. As we continue healing from prior family problems, we are learning how to communicate openly and respectfully

We expect to have a lot of fun by some of Minnesota's 10,000 lakes this summer. We will watch the Bald Eagles and Golden Eagles sitting in trees or soaring high in the sky, looking for roadkill. Countless Mallard Ducks and Canada Geese float past us, and various birds fly nearby, like Blue Birds, Swallows, Wrens, Goldfinches, and Hummingbirds. We will hear their songs all around us in these beautiful, peaceful places.

We recently got an inflatable kayak to get out on the lake. It's nice to float in the water, look at the fish swimming around, lily pads and white lily flowers with yellow centers, watch deer graze on the shoreline, and hear frogs croaking and birds flying and singing. My grandson expressed his gratitude for the Kayak and the fun we had in it. We also catch fish in a big net to look at and cast back.

Like my grandmother, I take my grandson out snow tubing

on Neil Park Hill during the winter. Life is simple and good! I'm passing down traditions.

I am very blessed! Ah, I am grateful for many blessings!

God is so good and trustworthy. He loves us, heals us, and restores us in everyday life when we seek Him. I need to be continually brought back to a healthy state of mind. Sometimes we take two steps forward and one step back, fighting to keep pressing ahead to better health mentally and physically.

CHAPTER 19
Looking Forward

Tia got a German Shepard puppy, and Ana got a Corgi puppy. I love seeing them all happy with their furry babies. Pets help heal and give people motivation toward better health. I highly recommend pets to people. The pet that best suits me is a rabbit the girls gave me for my birthday. I named her Bunz. Tia is great with matching pets with people's personalities. I love dogs, my Ana wanted to give me a dog for my birthday, but I would have been too anxious because I do not like to leave dogs behind to go to a job or anywhere. Bunz is easy to care for. She is happy to have a safe, quiet place to live. She has a mirror, fantastic fresh vegetables, and a hiding spot in her fenced-in area. I recently got her a very soft, furry bed and a tiny couch, just her size.

I have concluded that my life has amounted to something worthwhile. I hope it amounts to more in the future. It makes me cry to think about it! I have often forgiven my father that I would never amount to anything or be good for nothing. I must admit that I keep hoping and crying inside. It still gives me internal pain. I'm hoping the curses my dad gave me will be broken for good. Being silenced verbally only made me internalize my mental expressions through thought or writing. I pray to Almighty God that the curse from my father turns into my blessing! Our minds can possess a mighty and contagious force given by Our

Creator to positively impact each other in this world. I have learned to value my thoughts to bring solutions to life's given problems. Making something good out of tragedy is what we all can do!

One non-verbal message received from My Creator is, "I placed you people on this Earth where conditions are the safest compared to anywhere light-years away from you. Now take good care of each other! I have unconditional love for you, and please share that love!"

I want to communicate with victims and families, and friends of victims. Please contact me at:

WorthMoreThanAThousandWords.org

The End of Parole

I visit Dan and call or text him most days of any given month. He's been going through severe depression like he occasionally does. Law enforcement has taken away his computer, cell phone, and other items, including a sword and CDs. Dan tried to get his computer to run better and unknowingly deleted a monitor that watched what he was doing. Like most of us would be, he is lost without his devices. His two legal business plans that he told me about were in his computer files.

Pedos are supposed to allow monitoring of their computers and report all the devices they use. Dan informed me about convicted pedos that violate their parole rules and get tossed back into prison. Some violators have been caught with pornography, pictures, videos, etc., found on their computer and phone devices. Dan has heard firsthand about these seized items and stories in prison.

I asked questions about what he had on his computer that could be a problem. He confessed to me that he found pornography of Reese Whitherspoon as an adult that he copied to the computer. He said "adult," so I assume the law will find out for sure. I sent school pictures of the grandson that he downloaded. Since he was out of prison nearly five years ago, he has had no violations and has been successfully employed, working many overtime hours. He has been laid off recently, is on SSI, and is disabled. A roller walker aids his walking.

He was going through his possessions in case there was a search. He called to say I needed to come over right away. He gave no reason. I am currently stuck in a 9-5 job and must take care of my rest needs. The weather is snowy/icy. Also, my tires are a little worn. I couldn't make it to his place 45 minutes away. He asked God what to do about the antique family heirloom that his Grandfather Anderson had before the Civil War. It was a wooden bullet he said was worth a lot of money. Dan feared facing the possibility that he could go to federal prison for ten years if the law officials found it. He said God told him to get rid of it. He flushed it down the toilet! I yelled at him over the phone!"You took the girl's childhood from them, and now you took away their inheritance!" "This is God getting angry, using my voice!"I shouted. "I disobeyed God once, and I won't do it again," he defended. "You couldn't figure out how to get it to me?" I countered. He had time to drive it over to me if he wanted to. He could have put it in the crotch of a tree or under the mailbox!"You were thinking of number one again!" I yelled. I tell him off when I know he is wrong.

I have attended three talk sessions with people who help pedos get their heads on straighter. I have volunteered to be a "Pedo Watch Dog." I also ask my ex about any of his convicted friends: how they are doing and what they are doing. Some lead productive lives going in the right direction, and others go back to prison when they return to their old deviant groove.

Dan heard sirens and saw police officers at his door one week before parole was over. His heart was pounding hard and fast. He had been in suspense for weeks since his items were seized and in the process of being searched through. He thought he was going to prison for something that they found incriminating. An officer asked, "Did you call 9-1-1? "No," Dan replied with great relief. Someone upstairs in the apartment had called for help.

I was at Dan's apartment when his devices were returned to him. I was helping with moving furniture out of his apartment and helping get rid of expired cans of food. He got his computer and cell phone back and most of his CDs. He had Baby Metal CDs that detectives seized and a few young actors' and actresses' headshots that he had to delete. There was no reason for him to go to jail.

After his parole, I gave him a small bag of favorite candies and a card that said, "CONGRATULATIONS!" I wrote inside the card, "I want all good for you all the time and a great future of prosperity and success!" Dan smiled after receiving the gift and said, "Thank you!" He told his brother Joe who congratulated him too and tore up the several thousand-dollar check Dan sent by mail to him so he could take care of his money just in case he was sent to jail for something found on his devices.

I understand that Dan had some puzzling thoughts wondering why his daughters were still so angry with him. Are there any survivors of child sexual abuse that are happy that they were used and abused? Dan has admitted that he has learned more about person-to-person boundaries in his workbooks. He believes that in a few more years, it will be acceptable to allow pedos to be enmeshed with their victims as they please. I ask all former children who have been sexually abused: Is this going to be more acceptable? I am confident that most victims of child sexual abuse and people, in general, will not allow this behavior to ruin the lives of those who are so vulnerable.

Occasionally Dan and I discuss current events. He brought up the story about a young teen boy and his pre-teen cousin. He eventually asked with a puzzled expression. "How can you make love to someone and then kill them?" I listened intently to his statement. I'm learning how he thinks. He seems very confused about what I call "appropriate sexuality." In my book, appropriate sexuality involves mature, consenting individuals.

What am I to Dan? I simply want him to make the right choices from now on. I permanently lost my attraction to him the first moment I learned that he mistreated Tia and Ana. He believes we are friends. I think I'm more curious about how his head is screwed on than having him be my friend. I know I used to be a friend. Then I was a lover. Then I was a wife. No more! I am in love with answers and solutions to puzzling problems! I feel like I'm a watchdog. Yes! I much prefer being his watchdog but in a positive way! I am not entirely in control over his choices, but I believe he will never be able to spend time with any family members.

I say to all, "Question everything! It's healthy to do that!" I think there should be more volunteer pedo watchdogs out there. Perhaps there are.

RANDOM QUESTIONS:

Question: What do you think you needed when you were a child to help you not be inappropriately close to your much younger brother within your family growing up and the family you raised?

Answer: His mother scolded him when his little brother told her what he did. His mother called Daniel names like queer, etc.

Question: Do you think being taught about "no-touch" boundaries would have been helpful in your early life?

Answer: He learned about them while in group therapy with his favorite counselor. I asked if his much older sister had touched him inappropriately, and Dan said she didn't. Daniel explained that his Great Uncle Clyde exposed himself to Dan while he was wasting away in the nursing home, and he didn't know what he was doing.

Question: How many former sexually abused children who are now adults have you met that said they were happy to be inappropriately touched?

Answer: Dan explained that he found a guy on YouTube with a dog humping him who said this was his life.

Question: Did you ever think about the possibility that you'd be on the register of offenders before you acted on your deviant behavior?

Answer: He said he was trying to stop his inappropriate behavior, even asking God to help him. He still couldn't stop the behavior and prayed more about stopping the problem. It continued to be a struggle to end his deviant sexual behavior.

I would be happy to send any inquiry to Dan for those readers who have questions. Perhaps I can convince him to answer these perplexing questions for community service! You may also have questions to ask my daughters or me.

Please visit my website and send me any questions or comments:

WorthMoreThanAThousandWords.org